A Tale of Two Countries

A Tale of Two Countries:
Contemporary Fiction in English Canada and the United States

Stanley Fogel

ECW PRESS

Copyright © 1984 by ECW PRESS

CANADIAN CATALOGUING IN PUBLICATION DATA

Fogel, Stanley
    A tale of two countries

Bibliography: p.
ISBN 0-920802-49-4 (bound). – ISBN 0-920802-51-6 (pbk.)

1. Canadian fiction (English) – 20th century – History and criticism.* 2. American fiction – 20th
century – History and criticism. I. Title.

PS8199.F63   1984   813'.54'09   C84-099175-4
PR9192.5.F63   1984

A Tale of Two Countries has been published with the aid of a grant from the
University of St. Jerome's College, Waterloo Ontario. Additional grants have
been made available from the Ontario Arts Council and The Canada Council.

Typeset by Compeer; printed by Hignell; cover design by The Dragon's Eye Press.

Published by ECW PRESS, 307 Coxwell Avenue, Toronto Ontario.

Table of Contents

This book is dedicated to my parents.

Acknowledgements

Chapters One and Three contain a good many passages from the following article of mine: "Lost in the Canadian Funhouse" (*Queen's Quarterly*, Winter 1981). Chapter Two contains a good many passages from another article of mine, "Richard Nixon by Robert Coover, Roland Barthes by Roland Barthes" (*English Studies in Canada*, Summer 1982). Parts of Chapter Three were read at the Fifth International Conference on the Fantastic in the Arts as "Robert Kroetsch and the Canadian Fantastic." Another paper containing material from Chapter One was read at the Canadian Association of American Studies Conference, 1983, as "'Atlantis recedes; America grows.'"

The following people assisted me in various ways: Doug Letson and Rick Martin (who read much of the book and provided many helpful comments); Patti Anderson (who assisted me in proofreading as well as in preparing the notes); especially Laura Moyer (who typed the manuscript, taking an almost illegible script and transforming it into a series of drafts).

I am grateful to St. Jerome's College which provided the generous grant that made the publication of this book possible.

Prefatory Note

A Tale of Two Countries is a comparative study of American and Canadian fiction written in English and in the contemporary period. Although Robert Kroestch and George Bowering, most notably, have presented some insightful material on the topic, this is, I think, the first full-length venture of its kind. The two countries, despite their proximity and interaction, have produced two distinct kinds of fiction as well as two unassimilable modes of criticism. This book developed out of a curiosity about that situation, a curiosity augmented by university learning and teaching experiences in both countries.

Cathectic America: Anorectic Canada

THE RELATIONSHIP OF TWO COUNTRIES, especially two such as Canada and the United States which share the world's longest undefended common border, is a complex if not convoluted one. There are the common perceptions of what yokes and differentiates these two countries: a sense of the hegemony of the United States in all areas of Canadian life, its political, economic, and cultural dimensions; the complacency with which that is regarded south of the border, the acuteness with which it is registered north of it. To be American is to be barely aware of the Canadian sensibility; to be Canadian is to be obsessed by the American sensibility, especially insofar as it impinges on Canadians. This situation has led to the publication of a spate of Canadian works of all kinds, literary, journalistic, governmental, that seek to demarcate Canadian from American, to acknowledge and concomitantly to resist the monolith. "Now everything," writes Margaret Atwood in "Two-Headed Poems,"

> in the place is falling south
> into the dark pit left by Cincinnati after it crumbled.[1]

Although Kildare Dobbs frets over the difficulty of defining a Canadian sensibility — "the thought 'Canada' is impossible to think all at once"[2] — he writes a definition that at least distinguishes between Canada and the United States:

> There is still a powerful myth of the North. Against all evidence, Canadians sometimes like to think of themselves as a hardy, frugal race of "hommes du nord." For the farther north one goes, the farther one is from the United States and from supermarkets, superhighways, and advertising men in crew-cuts and two button suits.[3]

Despite the anachronistic quality of the invading advertising men and the uncommercialized landscape, the tenor of Dobbs's remarks is by no means untypical of Canada's stance to American inroads. In

"Global Pillage: The Economics of Commercial Television," Joyce Nelson cites the nefarious invasion into Canada of American television programs: "By being 'the easiest, best-paying customer' in the world, we're simply holding up, dutifully, a few sides of that American-built media box."[4] On all levels the dreaded miscegenation, dreaded, that is, by the more threatened of the two entities, has been and is being debated and frequently combatted. A Royal Commission report issued in the seventies entitled *To Know Ourselves* condemns the lack of Canadian content, human and otherwise, in Canadian universities; FIRA, the Foreign Investment Review Agency, was created to monitor all foreign, but primarily American, take-overs of Canadian business firms. The list of measures, proposed and taken, to impede American domination of Canada is, of course, much lengthier than the examples just cited.

That the debate and the setting of the limits of that debate are one-sided is not surprising. A hundred years ago, writes Stephen Spender in *Love-Hate Relations: English and American Sensibilities*, "Americans were much more concerned about their relations with the European culture than the English were with the American."[5] With the shift in power vis-à-vis England and America, that situation, as Spender makes clear, has been reversed. Insofar as Canadian and American relations are concerned, the balance of power has not shifted, nor is it ever likely to shift; consequently, Canadians will probably seek, far more often than Americans, to articulate the divergent, if they are indeed divergent, sensibilities of the two neighbours. If one of Jack Hicks's aperçus in his recent book on American contemporary fiction is any indication, America's grasp of the Canadian cultural scene will probably remain fuzzy. Among the women he cites as writing substantial fiction he includes Margaret Atwood who, he affirms, has gained an international reputation and "who writes across the border in Quebec...."[6]

To return to Spender's book, it is interesting insofar as this study is concerned to note that *Love-Hate Relations* is part of a noble lineage of works that define the American character in opposition to the English or old world one, which it resisted and from which it broke. More specifically Spender, as does D.H. Lawrence in *Studies in Classic American Literature* before him and Peter Conrad in *Imagining America* after him, reads the opposed sensibilities largely from the literary output of England and the United States. ("The Anglo-American relationship with which I am here concerned is, for the most part, literary" [Spender, p. xv].) Alexis de Tocqueville's *Democracy in*

America, though more encyclopaedic in its focus, is an eminent precursor of this mode. De Tocqueville's summation of the literary scene in America as it existed *circa* 1830 does not call for an extended comparison or extrapolation: "The inhabitants of the United States have then, at present, properly speaking, no literature. The only authors whom I acknowledge as American are the journalists. They indeed are not great writers, but they speak the language of their country, and make themselves heard. Other authors are alien...."[7] Later surveyors of American literature find far greater plenitude, usually seeing in that literature an energy and vitality that contrast especially sharply with the more genteel and decorous tradition of British literature. Atavistically inclined Lawrence, who referred to Whitman as a white aboriginal, is far more enamoured of the qualities of America and American literature than is Spender. At the end of his book Spender reveals his hope that "perhaps the English can maintain distance and sanity" (Spender, p. 318).

Not all contemporary critical statements by the English contain such a staunch sense of the inviolability and attractiveness of the British tradition and of contemporary British literature. Indeed *Granta*, sub-titled the new series from Cambridge, finds the current state of British fiction fusty in the extreme. The first two issues feature so-called experimental American writers such as William Gass, Donald Barthelme, Ronald Sukenick, Robert Coover, and John Barth. *Granta 3* presents a symposium on the British novel provocatively called "The End of the English Novel." In a piece entitled "An Irrelevant Parochialism," Frederick Bowers launches a diatribe against the complacency of the contemporary British novel:

> ... its conformity, its traditional sameness, and its realistically rendered provincialism. Shaped only by its contents, the British novel is the product of group mentality: local, quaint, and self-consciously xenophobic. Why is it that of the many able craftsmen writing in Britain so few have experimented with form, and, of those, experimented with such caution?[8]

Bowers' attack is reiterated by *Granta*'s editor, Bill Buford, whose introduction to the third issue lacerates English timidity and insularity. "The American writer's sense of experiment is largely the consequence of participating in an international dialogue."[9]

That dialogue, spawned by Joyce's logodaedaly and refined by the precepts and fictions of Vladimir Nabokov and Jorge Luis Borges, who might properly be called the fathers of experimental fiction, has been virulently engaged in by contemporary French writers, those practitioners of the *nouveau roman* such as Alain Robbe-Grillet, Michel Butor, and Nathalie Sarraute; by contemporary South American writers, Borgesian fabulators such as Julio Cortazar, Manuel Puig, and José Donoso; by contemporary American writers, metafictionists such as John Barth, Donald Barthelme, Robert Coover, Kurt Vonnegut, and William Gass, among many others. (It should be noted that the term "metafiction" was coined by Gass in an essay called "Philosophy and the Form of Fiction." Simply stated, until further extrapolation in the section in Chapter Two dealing with Gass, the major premise of metafiction is that none of the conventions of fiction or reality is sacrosanct.) Buford finds no such dialogue and no such strain of literature flourishing in the British Isles. He quotes approvingly the former editor of *TriQuarterly*, Charles Newman, under whose direction that journal published some of the finest avant-garde literature, both American (in a series called "Ongoing American Fiction") and foreign: "'There is a movement of younger writers...to learn unselfconsciously from national literatures other than their own. There are very few promising and or young American writers today who have not been more influenced by "foreign" writing than by any of their immediate predecessors'" (Buford, p.9). Regretting the seeming lack of awareness of Joyce, Nabokov, and Borges on the part of his countrymen, Buford gives a specific example of British parochialism. G. Cabrera Infante's *Three Trapped Tigers*, he writes, was published in Great Britain in 1980, fifteen years after it was written and ten years after it was published in the United States. He queries, "Is it really surprising that a book of this sort, written over fifteen years ago, should be dismissed here—when at last it does appear—as an-oh-yes-another-one-of-those?" (Buford, p. 10).

It is here that the English-American literary debate finds its parallel in the Canadian-American situation. In an interview given to me recently, Harold Horwood, past president of the Canadian Writers' Union and author of such works as *The Colonial Dream: 1497–1760* and *White Eskimo: A Novel of Labrador*, said that the current period will, in years to come, be regarded as the Canadian renaissance in which Canada's seminal literary texts were being written and published. This period is akin to the 1850s in the United States, which were labelled the American renaissance by F. O. Matthiessen in *American Renaissance: Art and Expression in the Age of Emerson and Whitman*. Given that these are the halcyon years, Horwood asserted

4

that foreign models, especially American ones, were no longer needed in the creative-writing course that he taught at the University of Waterloo in conjunction with another faculty member. For him American models would inculcate American styles of living as well as writing. Because Canadians are a less violent people than Americans, Horwood said wittily, their writers need not be cast in a suicidal mould such as John Kennedy Toole was. (Toole's *A Confederacy of Dunces* was published posthumously and won the 1981 Pulitzer Prize for fiction.) For Horwood, Toole's mode of dying was Hemingway-like.

Canadian Literature in the 70's, edited by Paul Denham and Mary Jane Edwards, perpetuates the isolationist and perhaps claustrophobic context in which contemporary Canadian literature is written and read. Denham and Edwards go so far as to find in nationalistic literature evidence of maturity, of a burgeoning sureness of identity, rather than evidence of an adolescent or a nascent literature:

> In the 1970's Canadian writers still addressed themselves to international audiences, but the process no longer seemed as essential to Canada's cultural maturity as it once did, and too great an emphasis on its importance was sometimes seen as a hold-over from a colonial past. Perhaps, in fact, a writer cannot be a good internationalist and a good nationalist without being a good regionalist; for it seems essential that the creative writer have a strong sense of his own time and place.[10]

In an international critical and aesthetic climate that gives wide currency to the witticism, "God wasn't a bad novelist, but he was a realist," that Barth uttered in a 1965 interview featured in *Wisconsin Studies in Contemporary Literature* [6, No. 1 (Winter-Spring 1965)] and which has created a cause célèbre out of Jacques Derrida and his acolytes who insist on the anti-referential nature of language, literary and otherwise, the criterion of being a good regionalist seems not merely isolationist, but also irrelevant. As a sop to the technicians of the novel and other genres, Denham and Edwards confidently and facilely assert that "the form of much poetry, fiction, and drama in Canada in the 1970's was innovative" (Denham and Edwards, p. xx). Insofar as fiction writing is concerned, the reader of *Canadian Literature in the 70's* is advised that contemporary Canadian short-story writers de-emphasize plot and character, shifting their focuses to texture, tone, and atmosphere. "The Canadian writers' concern for such qualities as texture and tone was closely related to the preoccupa-

tion of much contemporary literature with rendering details of particular places and times" (Denham and Edwards, p. xxi). Ignoring, if one
can, the wrongheadedness of such a generalization about the penchant
of contemporary literature for verisimilitude, one can legitimately ask
how so reactionary a statement about the direction of contemporary
literature can be proffered by anyone who has read outside of the limits
of Canadian literature and who has discerned what is more than a
localized movement on the part of fiction writers and critical theorists
away from mimetic notions of art and traditional notions of criticism.
One can also legitimately ask about the context of Canadian fiction,
which fosters such parochial concerns.

What with all the anxiety in Canadian cultural and political spheres
about American influence, it is clear that Canadian fiction and its
attendant theoretical context appear, anomalously, to have escaped
any American or, via the American, continental intrusion, much less
subsumption. In and of itself this situation is intriguing and merits a
full study. There are other reasons, however, equally as important that
call for a comparative study of contemporary fiction and theory of
fiction in Canada and the United States. The first is, surprisingly, that
it has rarely been done before and never to my knowledge in a full-
length study. A few disparate facets of the relationship are examined in
issue number 22 of *Essays on Canadian Writing*. Also, *Mosaic: A
Journal for the Interdisciplinary Study of Literature*, from the University of Manitoba, did issue a special number in the spring of 1981
called "Beyond Nationalism: The Canadian Literary Scene in Global
Perspective." A few of the articles, most notably a preface by Robert
Kroetsch and an essay by Sherrill Grace that compares one of
Kroetsch's novels with one of Thomas Pynchon's, briefly examine
contrasting tendencies on the part of Canadian and American writers
of fiction. In "The Canadian Writer and the American Literary
Tradition," another piece that relates directly to the issue at hand and
which predates the *Mosaic* number by some ten years, Kroetsch notes
that Canadians and Americans have had to confront an identical
linguistic situation: "Historically, both Canadians and Americans
have experienced the task of commencing a new literature in a
mandarin language."[11] Thus, the two responses of these countries,
which exist in close proximity to one another, can be instructively
compared. The second reason for this study is that Canadian and
American sensibilities can be as sharply and incisively delineated in the
comparison, as the English and American sensibilities are in part
clarified by Spender in *Love-Hate Relations*. The third is that the

debate about the relative strengths and weaknesses of the British novel, matched with those of the American novel, could be profitably conducted by Canadian literati interested in an other than inbred appreciation of Canadian literature.

That it is appropriate the study be undertaken by a Canadian is obvious, again extrapolating from Spender's remarks about the concern now shown by the British about their relations with Americans. American critics have defined and redefined the contemporary American sensibility as it is manifested in American fiction. In *Victims: Textual Strategies in Recent American Fiction*, Paul Bruss encapsulates contemporary American fiction as, in Roland Barthes's terminology, "writerly" rather than "readerly," that is to say ludic or playful rather than mimetic or didactic, and discusses Nabokov, Barthelme, and Jerzy Kosinski in this context. In *Readings from the New Book of Nature: Physics and Metaphysics in the Modern Novel* Robert Nadeau examines the work of among others, Barth, Thomas Pynchon, and Vonnegut, in the context of modern physics. Hicks, in *In the Singer's Temple*, treats various contemporary American writers who represent, he feels, various isolated communities (black, pop, metafictive, feminist). These are just a few of the very recent assessments. Earlier books were written by critics such as Robert Scholes who dealt with contemporary fabulation in *The Fabulators*, Charles Harris who dealt with contemporary fiction of the absurd in *Contemporary American Novelists of the Absurd*, and Raymond Olderman who read the protagonists in contemporary American fiction as late inhabitants of Eliot's "wasteland" in *Beyond the Wasteland: The American Novel in the Nineteen-Sixties*. All of these writers, with varying degrees of dexterity, shuffle around the foremost contemporary American writers — Barth, Barthelme, Pynchon, Ken Kesey — to provide a sense of the state of the art and concomitantly a state of the state. Their work would probably not have been augmented significantly by the introduction of Canadian materials, given the panoply of events and ideas that America has spawned or spewed, both metaphorically and literally, in the past thirty years. With perhaps two exceptions — Chief Bromden's planned escape to Canada at the end of Kesey's *One Flew Over the Cuckoo's Nest* and Germaine Pitt's tryst with her mysterious and elusive Castine at the Walper Hotel in Kitchener, Ontario, somewhere in the labyrinthine passages of Barth's *Letters* — the Canadian presence in American fiction is non-existent. An "Imagining Canada," along the lines of Conrad's *Imagining America*, except in terms of the popular percep-

7

tion of a frozen tundra, would probably not be longer than a haiku poem. Thus, an American investigation of the two countries' sensibilities and fictions would be a highly unlikely or at least highly idiosyncratic venture.

Nonetheless, the enterprise is a worthwhile one: not to extirpate further the American presence from Canadians' midst; not to demand attention from an American readership for Canadian literature, though that would not be an unattractive by-product. Rather, the study merits consideration because the recent fictions of Canadian writers and those of writers in the United States are, for the most part, sharply divergent in form and content; this itself provides some unique insights into the two countries. As will be expatiated upon in greater detail in the pages which follow, the formalist or metafictive concerns that have dominated the pages of *TriQuarterly* and *American Review* and the novels of Barth, Barthelme, Coover, Gass, Pynchon, and other writers of metafiction are almost completely absent in Canadian journals and in the works of prominent and even for the most part peripheral Canadian writers of fiction. Why is this the case and what does it reveal about Canadian letters and the Canadian climate of opinion in general? To reverse the question and give it more relevance to American literary and social contexts, why has metafiction, experimental fiction that places form in the foreground and is decidedly anti-mimetic, gained so many American practitioners? Despite the fact that, as suggested above, answers to this last question have been tendered by a phalanx of American critics, a comparative study of the phenomenon may provide answers that have not previously been given.

Northrop Frye asked a seemingly innocent question, "Where is here?" He answered his own question by asserting that the Canadian "here" is a more inchoate place, physically and culturally, than the American "here":

> ...apparently we're still in the process of taking inventories and rendering accounts....
>
> We came into this century without any agreement on what kind of people we were — or even, whether a Canadian could be identified.
>
> Nine-tenths of our land mass existed as a kind of vague miasma.[12]

Frye goes on to say in "Journey without Arrival, a Personal Point of View," a television program in the "Images of Canada" series, that the condition just stated is beginning to change. He assigns a vital role in that process to the Canadian artists, "the people who have followed Pratt, the Earle Birneys, the Margaret Atwoods, and James Reaneys," calling them "the mapmakers of the Canadian imagination."[13] Clearly, the Canadian artist is assigned a meaningful role in formulating a Canadian identity. The tone and the direction of Frye's remarks are far different from the ringing final comment of the narrator in Robert Coover's play "Love Scene": "Imagination rules the world, shithead!"[14] As the section devoted to Coover will, I hope, make abundantly clear, the role of the American writer according to Coover and many others is antagonistic rather than supportive; his notion is that the artist must deconstruct rather than construct.

These antinomies, deconstruct and construct, are extremely important to the chapters which follow. Indeed, it is important to the premise of this introduction: cathectic America is a country that has, in the minds and works of most of its pre-eminent writers of fiction, reified and rigidified many of the attitudes, values, and symbols that have coalesced as the American identity; anorectic Canada is a country which has not yet, in the minds and works of its most pre-eminent writers of fiction (as well as most of its government officials and citizens), formed and sustained those same entities, both concrete and abstract, that give a country its definitive and distinctive character. The word, "deconstruction," of course, has explicit theoretical and by now ideological overtones. Deconstruction refers to Derrida's attempts to undo metaphysical schema or constructs, to demonstrate the flimsiness of the overviews and arguments as well as the logocentrism of the Western world's foremost philosophers. It devalues and denigrates, among other concepts, idealism, transcendence, self, and origin. One of the reasons, I think, for the popularity of Derrida and what have been called his poststructuralist writings as well as the work of his numerous disciples, such as J. Hillis Miller and Geoffrey Hartman, whom he has garnered in the United States, is that Derrida's method of deconstruction has many affinities with the experiments of the metafictionists. Both tend to undo holistic, integrated modes of understanding the world. In addition to the specialized meaning of deconstruction for this study, then, the word also implies the undermining of established meaning generally, whereas construction entails the opposite, the creation and development of such meaning.

Probably more dramatically than any other country, America has

9

imagined and created itself as a distinctive and forceful entity. The sense of the United States is vastly different from the synopsis offered by Frye of an ill-defined, indistinct Canada. On the occasion of America's bicentennial Irving Howe begins his lead essay in *The New York Times Book Review* with the following:

> With America, a new idea comes into the world; with American literature, a new voice. As a dream or fantasy of overburdened Europeans, the idea can be heard even before the Atlantic settlements. It flourishes a while later in the colonies themselves, among Puritan divines, through the letters of the farmer Crevecoeur, amid the reflections of Thomas Jefferson. It speaks of a second Israel through God's provision, or in secular language, of a social compact forged by sturdy freeholders. And it depends on a common yielding to the myth of a new start for humanity on unsullied ground.[15]

This idea of America, because of its mythopoeic dimensions, was securely established even before the country was. For John Locke, in Edenic terms, in the beginning all the world was America; for William Blake in "America: A Prophecy" the country takes on an apocalyptic and ecstatic configuration; for Samuel Taylor Coleridge it was a place to establish an ideal society, a Pantisocracy to be created on the banks of the Susquehanna. The magnitude of the myth impels D.H. Lawrence to write *Studies in Classic American Literature* in which he reveals America sloughing off the accretions of and by extension, for Lawrence, the detritus of civilization. Of "The Leather-stocking Tales" he writes: "[The Tales] go backwards, from old age to golden youth. That is the true myth of America. She starts old, old, wrinkled and writhing in an old skin. And there is a gradual sloughing off of the old skin, towards a new youth."[16] His departure from England for New Mexico is his personal response to that myth.

With both beneficent and deleterious consequences, the myth has taken hold of and shaped the American character. The New World was thought to be a place, a space, in which to create a utopia. "The United States themselves," wrote Walt Whitman, "are essentially the greatest poem."[17] Poem and place were the exemplars of the American dream: "Zealots, malcontents, entrepreneurs, the early settlers were a self-selecting group of dreamers who implanted in the New World a sense of optimism and fierce ambition to make life in such inhospitable terrain equal to their dreams.... A society inventing itself."[18] The power of F. Scott Fitzgerald's *The Great Gatsby* comes from Gatsby's attempt to anthropomorphize that dream, his heroic attempt to invent or shape himself ("Jay Gatsby...sprang from his Platonic conception of himself"),[19] a fictional synecdoche for the country's endeavour. Nick's lament at the end of the novel is not for Gatsby, but for the Gatsby who represented a country that once was "the old island here that flowered...for Dutch sailors' eyes — a fresh, green breast of the new world."[20] It is a paean to the potential that America had, to the myth that it strove to embody.

Not only Gatsby and other fictional characters but also American historical personages have been subject to the same inflation. In *Lindbergh Alone* there is featured at the beginning of the book a photograph of the airfield from which Lindbergh embarked on his historic flight across the Atlantic; at the end of the book is a photograph of a boy on a raft. Lindbergh's achievement becomes mythified: the unaided self, the ideal individual, the pioneering American are all subsumed in and represented by the man. Brendan Gill, the author of *Lindbergh Alone*, not only quotes popular magazines of the time which articulate this myth-related status, he also inflates it himself. "Lindbergh would have been at home in Twain's pre-Civil War environment....He stood for the promises of applied science as a young poet might stand for the promises of the word. He had a thrilling gospel to preach...."[21] John Alcock and Arthur Brown, two Newfoundlanders, performed the transatlantic flight almost a decade before Lindbergh did. This attests not to the relative merits of the persons involved but to the Americans' faculty for myth-making and to the absence of such a Canadian attribute. One only has to think of early Americans such as Davy Crockett and Daniel Boone and compare their stature with that of Radisson and Groseilliers, two early explorers of Canada, to solidify one's sense of the diametrically opposed ways Americans and Canadians create their respective histories. No doubt in response to the popularity of shows celebrating Davy Crockett, the Canadian Broadcasting Corporation developed a television series on Radisson and Groseilliers. The series is memorable only for the proleptic hydro poles and airplanes that were accidentally recorded by the show's cameras.

Deconstruction of Western heroes is not required in Canada because their heroic-mythic characteristics were never constructed in the first place. On the other hand, an American movie such as Robert Altman's *Buffalo Bill and the Indians or Sitting Bull's History Lesson* engages in just such an activity. Paul Newman's Buffalo Bill puts on his heroic stature when he puts on his make-up. The producer of Buffalo Bill's Wild West Show boasts that he is going to "Cody-fy" the world. Many unsympathetic America watchers would probably proclaim that this is an American paradigm. History for Altman is clearly something that has been shaped, constructed, and codified and is clearly in need of the reconstruction that might follow deconstruction. At one point in the film, Bill upbraids Sitting Bull when the latter asks that his act be a dramatization of American soldiers murdering unarmed Indian women and children. He just wants to show the truth to the people says a sympathetic Annie Oakley. Says Bill, I have a better sense of history.

With an irreverence akin to Altman's, contemporary American writers of fiction provide an equally jaundiced sense of history. Indeed, Vonnegut's *Breakfast of Champions: Or Goodbye, Blue Monday* and Barth's *The Sot-Weed Factor* seek clearly and emphatically to reduce American history to the status of fiction. As the narrator of *Breakfast of Champions* utters wryly,

> teachers of children in the United States of America wrote this date on blackboards again and again...1492.
> The teachers told the children that this was when their continent was discovered by human beings. Actually, millions of human beings were already living full and imaginative lives on the continent in 1492. That was simply the year in which sea pirates began to cheat and rob and kill them.[22]

It is also relevant to mention here the contemporary American fiction writers' preoccupation with working genuinely historical personages into their works. Coover's *The Public Burning*, which will be dealt with later in much greater detail, features Richard Nixon and Ethel Rosenberg primarily; E.L. Doctorow's *The Book of Daniel* also deals with the Rosenbergs. Barthelme's Robert Kennedy in "Robert Kennedy Saved from Drowning," Joseph Heller's Henry Kissinger in *Good as Gold*, and the characters of lesser known writers such as Max Apple's Fidel Castro, Gerald Ford and Howard Johnson in *The Oranging of America*, and Frederic Tuten's Mao in *The Adventures of Mao on the Long March* are a few of the many historical figures who people contemporary American novels and short stories. (As an aside, which nonetheless affirms my thesis that Canadian and American tendencies regarding myth-making are antithetical, the most notable Canadian attempt to deconstruct an historical figure is Michael

Ondaatje's *The Collected Works of Billy the Kid: Left Handed Poems* which subjects American lore to the scrutiny of fiction.) What has been created by these writers is a unique genre, a new kind of historical fiction, one that is not interested in verisimilitude, the texture of reality that traditionally legitimizes more orthodox historical fiction. On the contrary, dissatisfied with cathectic America, with among other things the *kitsch*-art industry, which has grown up around the assassinated Kennedy brothers, Coover, Barthelme, and the other writers of metafiction attempt to lacerate inflated, revered historical images. They are disenchanted with the ideological miasma which has surrounded and contributed to events such as the Rosenberg executions, the McCarthy blacklistings, and the firebombing of Dresden. More aptly, they set out to deconstruct the palpably fictive or artificial quality of the figures and events they bring into the ambit of their fictions. They do this by exaggerating the historical tableau or otherwise rendering it extravagantly stylized.

For Ihab Hassan, who reads America in mythopoeic terms, there is a dialectic which captures the American sensibility that he calls "America and Atlantis": "Wherever Atlantis may have been or will be, some say that the energy of American illusion helps to discover it — and to corrupt it."[23] This dialectic encapsulates the contradiction between the possibilities America contains and the actualities that are created. While Pittsburgh may seem so unlike Utopia that one would think the dream has been rendered extinct, that is not the case. Despite an inevitable condition in which "Atlantis recedes; America grows" (Hassan, p. 176), both the ideal and the real persist in and account for the vitality of the American experience. This is so because, as Hassan divulges, "within the moist, dark imagination, men and women still seek alternative realities.... They seek, beyond 'struggling afflictions,' Blake's prophecy of America: 'another portion of the infinite'" (Hassan, p. 176). Such a locale is more metaphorical than literal.

Nonetheless, as Jane Kramer reveals in *The Last Cowboy*, despite the realization of a concrete (in both senses of the word) Pittsburgh, the myth persists tenaciously. Henry Blanton, the eponymous last cowboy, is of the genuine rather than the newly minted urban variety; or at least he is genuine insofar as he accepts the implantation of the myth in the American West. He has ingested the tenets of the cowboy that were celebrated by then President Carter in a statement on the death of John Wayne in which he said that John Wayne was bigger than life: In an age of few heroes, he was the genuine article. In *John Wayne: A Tribute* Wayne is given the following epitaph: "John Wayne the movie star lives on as a screen symbol of an American legend: the masculine, plain-talking man of action, quick with his hands or his gun, incorruptible and always on the side of right."[24] Blanton's values which Kramer enumerates are those of a "proper" cowboy, a John Wayne-like figure, shaped, Kramer maintains, by urban Easterners' myths:

> He became for those Easterners the frontier's custodian. They made him Rousseau's Emile with a six gun. They turned man-in-nature into a myth of natural man, and added natural justice to ease the menace of a place that lay beyond their hegemony and their institutions. They saw to it that he was born good, and that if he died violently, he died wise and defiant and uncorrupted. They set him against outlaws and spoilers, card sharks and Comanches.[25]

The American dream is not merely a composite of cowboy or rural myths. It is revivified in a work as engaged with the modern technological universe as is *Zen and the Art of Motorcycle Maintenance: An Inquiry into Values*. Robert Pirsig's prescription in *Zen* is for a world that recognizes the art in technology. ("Actually a root word of technology, *techne*, originally *meant* 'art.':'")[26] In Pirsig's quirky vocabulary the expression of quality in the worker's and consumer's commitment to whatever he makes or uses is enough to resuscitate the American dream. Also, despite the fact that Americans have been shaken by the *domestic* results of their engagement in Vietnam and by their sense of vulnerability precipitated by the oil embargo of the mid-seventies, there is a sense on the part of the writers of metafiction that enough ideological reification has occurred that deconstruction must still be performed. John Updike's Rabbit might sigh nostalgically about "decades when Americans moved within the American dream, laughing at it, starving on it, but living it, humming it, the national anthem everywhere";[27] however, for the writers of metafiction, to cite Hassan with whom they would agree, America has "made greedy, deadly history" (Hassan, p. 176) in the past few decades. Moreover, their perception is that the American character has hardened, has rigidified into seeming naturalness — a naturalness that their fictions make abundantly clear is *not* natural; it is ideological and perniciously so at that.

Obsession with the American dream is not a mid- to late-twentieth-century phenomenon; nor is it solely the metafictionists' preoccupation. Theodore Dreiser's *An American Tragedy*, Edward Albee's *The American Dream*, and Allen Ginsberg's "America" challenge, in various ways, all facile assumptions that in America the ideal has been embodied in the real, that, in the lexicon used earlier, Pittsburgh is indeed Utopia. Most pithily Allen Ginsberg struts a persona inimical to the mainstream American dream:

> America I feel sentimental about the Wobblies.
> America I used to be a communist when I was a kid I'm not sorry.
> I smoke marijuana every chance I get....
> You should have seen me reading Marx.
> My psychoanalyst thinks I'm perfectly right.
> I won't say the Lord's Prayer.[28]

Even though assaults on the American identity have been diverse in terms of tone — tenacious, vitriolic, or, in the case of Ginsberg's "America," flippant — after all, some of Melville's trenchant nastiness in *Moby-Dick: Or, The Whale* had the same target — the metafictionist assault is a unique one, one that has a unique epistemological perspective. John Gardner's histrionics in *On Moral Fiction* are misplaced in their accusation that metafiction is fiction that is merely play with language, that it can be characterized as academic, portentous, opaque, sterile, misanthropic, perverse, and shallow. Certainly the metafictionist does not neutrally accept the conventions of fiction, the importance of plot, character, theme, and setting; certainly, also, the metafictionist does not passively accept language as a window onto the world. However, the fiction of Coover and Gass is often explicitly engagé and that of Barth and Barthelme, among others, is in no way remote from the main currents of American life. Indeed, the work of the metafictionist, in terms of both content *and* form, has a political thrust — it is saturated with the notion that the American character is a construct, a bad fiction. Not only is America not accorded absolute status, but the means of making fiction are also not inviolable. Metafiction is, after all, fiction that explores the theory of fiction.

Regardless of its predominantly theoretical focus, metafiction is highly committed fiction, especially if one accepts Sartre's notion that any technique implies a metaphysic. One of the misconceptions about contemporary American fiction, at least that kind of fiction which I would maintain is most seminal in this period, is that it is fabular or fantastical, that it eschews realism, because the reality of contemporary America is too awesome, too bizarre to capture successfully in fiction. Mas'ud Zavarzadeh quotes a *New Republic* reviewer who writes, "The America of 1965, with its assassinations, torched ghettos, campus wars, crime waves, alienations, deposed kings and crazed pretenders, almost seems too much for a single book. Offered as a novel, it might be rejected even by the lowliest of publishing house readers."[29] Zavarzadeh relates an anti-war rally's attempted levitation of the Pentagon and other such events as if these events are too absurd to be embellished, as if the transcription of them usurps the novelist's role. Hicks, in *In the Singer's Temple*, avers similarly that he agrees with Alvin Toffler's *Future Shock:* "the magnitude and rate of change [have] created, however temporarily, a society unable to cope psychically" (Hicks, p. 7). Thus, Hicks writes, "I find it scarcely odd that the young, earliest victims of future shock, choose neither to treat it nor to project its causes in their fiction" (Hicks, p. 7). Not only did the young not have to confront immediately Dachau, Auschwitz, Belsen, Hiroshima, Nagasaki — far truer traumas; but they also, in their portrayal of the historical personages enumerated earlier and in the investigation of an American landscape palpably fantastical, but genuinely established, do investigate, and for the most part undermine, a country that is interpretable, no matter how diverse and seemingly inexplicable its actions and characters. Coover finds fantastical the ambience surrounding the Rosenbergs' executions and the executions themselves. He extrapolates from the events and has Gene Autry sing "Back in the Saddle Again" at the executions. The metafictionist tries to examine the sensibility that accounts for such bizarre actual events.

Ironically, George Steiner, in an unrelentingly disdainful assessment of American cultural life that he contributed to a *Salmagundi* symposium, presents an antithetical argument for what he regards as the truncated power of contemporary American fiction. Great art, argues Steiner, is produced only in a place which is under stress, at a time which is stressful; it is produced "under conditions of individual *anomie,* of anarchic or even pathological unsociability and in contexts of political autocracy.... 'Censorship is the mother of metaphor,' notes Borges."[30] Thus, for Steiner American fiction cannot have the intensity and meaningfulness of the works of such writers as Aleksandr Zinoviev, Aleksandr Solzhenitsyn, and Eugene Pasternak. Steiner seems to me to be as erroneous in holding this position as Hicks and Zavarzadeh are in holding theirs. There are two clichéd and misconceived notions held by him. The first is that contemporary literature cannot have the stature and nobility of earlier literatures; the second is that European literature deserves greater reverence than North American literature. (The oracular utterance, Shakespeare, for all that portends not intrinsically in terms of the plays, but rather as it adumbrates culture, good breeding, the cognoscenti, is a staple of many academics in English departments and other cultural institutions.)

For E.L. Doctorow, for instance, whose writing is highly politicized, the language of literature is subversive regardless of the country in which it has been produced. His insightful essay, "False Documents," develops the argument that one can descry two languages: one is a language of the regime and the other is a language of freedom. Paraphrasing George Orwell's contention that sanity is statistical, Doctorow finds in democracies an ideological straitjacket as oppressive as that imposed by totalitarian states. He writes:

> What we proclaim as the discovered factual world can be challenged as the questionable world we ourselves have painted — the cultural museum of our values, dogmas, assumptions, that prescribes for us not only what we may like and dislike, believe and disbelieve, but also what we may be permitted to see and not to see.[31]

Doctorow's suspicion of "the real world," of realism, scientific methodology, the social sciences, as well as their attendant languages which for him are the language of the regime, is endemic to the writer of metafiction. For Gass, Doctorow's kindred spirit in this regard, philosophy has gained false status from its affiliation with the language of the regime; Gass seeks to ally it with fiction stating that "the novelist can learn more from the philosopher who has been lying longer.... The soul, we must remember, is the philosopher's invention, as thrilling a creation as, for instance, Madame Bovary."[32] Doctorow similarly seeks to reduce or alter history's status claiming that many of the key trials in United States court history have derived their truth from the language of the regime rather than from certifiable reality; he mentions Scopes, Sacco and Vanzetti, the Rosenbergs. Thus, Doctorow yokes the disciplines that have been accorded legitimacy, that have been accepted as hard currency in the real world, ethics, psychology, sociology, with the fiction maker's products. They are, for him, all false documents: "but we [novelists] are to be trusted because

17

ours is the only profession forced to admit that it lies — and that bestows upon us the mantle of honesty."[33]

This paradox is the central premise out of which the contemporary American novelist writes. Awareness and assimilation of it make for neither a sterile academic exercise, nor a politically irrelevant text. It provides a recognition that the American identity as well as the events that identity has influenced or perpetrated is a rigidified, a verified construct, one which deserves exposure as a false document. Experimental fiction embodied in the works of such authors as Coover, Gass, Barth, and Barthelme combats the language of the regime because that force's power dictates criteria for what Doctorow would call patently false documents. Such literature can also be subversive, as Alain Robbe-Grillet points out in his manifesto for untraditional fiction, *For a New Novel*, especially insofar as it undermines the reader's traditional approach to fiction. What the avant-garde novelist demands of the reader is "no longer to receive ready-made a world completed, full, closed upon itself, but on the contrary to participate in a creation, to invent in his turn the work — and the world — and thus to learn to invent his own life."[34]

That experimental fiction is a peripheral strain of the contemporary Canadian novel is easier to understand given the lack of a perceived identity to deconstruct. Canada's identity — the Canadian constitution was sent to Britain's parliament for approval at the close of 1981 — is still inchoate. Frye's contention that America has created a much firmer sense of its own identity, complete with landmarks, dates, and historical events, is echoed, as I stated earlier, by many Canadian writers and politicians. In a crisis-edged way, for instance, Atwood has taken up Frye's challenging question, "Where is here?" She writes that literature is vital in articulating our "here"; it creates a map, a geography of the mind, which defines us, which demarcates "who and where we have been. We need such a map desperately, we need to know about here, because here is where we live. For the members of a country or a culture, shared knowledge of their place, their here, is not a luxury but a necessity. Without that knowledge we will not survive."[35] Kroetsch in his *Mosaic* "Prologue" to "Beyond Nationalism: The Canadian Literary Scene in Global Perspective" agrees that this is a seminal quest for modern Canadian writers; moreover, in "The Canadian Writer and the American Literary Tradition" he argues that this kind of question was vital to the nineteenth-century American writer. One sees most notably in Whitman's paean to the English language and the American land mass in his "Preface" to *Leaves of Grass* and in Melville's explicit attempt in *Moby-Dick* to wed Shakespearean nobility to American whalers, a desire to develop a notion of the distinctiveness of American literature and American life. In current Canadian literature Kroetsch finds the search for identity to be paramount: "in novel after novel, the quest is, implicitly or even explicitly, genealogical."[36] Again, casting a look backwards at James Fenimore Cooper's *The Last of the Mohicans* or Mark Twain's *Adventures of Huckleberry Finn*, one sees the mid-nineteenth-century American concern for roots, for lineage. In the case of *The Last of the Mohicans* the reader follows Duncan Heyward's transition from Englishman lost in the forest to American taming it; in the case of *Huckleberry Finn* the reader observes Huck Finn trying to evade any civilized legacy. Regardless, in both books the quest is genealogical.

A comparison of contemporary literature in English Canada and the United States reveals a startling disparity in the two perceptions of here. Here for American writers is a monolith, often named, which must be combatted, reviled, or exorcised. The American here comes with a clearly formed set of characteristics and an apparently universally grasped ideology. Canada's here is rarely named in the pages of contemporary Canadian writers; it cannot be named. (The name, "Canada," it has been speculated, comes from an Indian word meaning "there is nothing here," or "we do not understand.") This is not to say that place names and regions are not mentioned and described; of course they are. However, the ideological baggage, which goes with the United States, does not encumber Canada. The latter country, therefore, is not the object of writers' thrusts or assaults. In her insightful study of Kroetsch's *Badlands* and Pynchon's *The Crying of Lot 49* in the "Beyond Nationalism" issue of *Mosaic*, Sherrill Grace provides an example of the palpable difference the identities of the two countries project. Oedipa, the heroine of Pynchon's novel, is faced with unravelling the legacy of Pierce Inverarity whose sprawling, labyrinthine network of corporations turns out to be America itself; she says its legacy is America. Oedipa is overwhelmed searching for some other place, some style of living other than the dominant one. "Another mode of meaning behind the obvious or none,"[37] she utters fatefully. She is doomed never to discover that mode. Such a claustrophobic context is non-existent in *Badlands* in which Anna is far freer than is Oedipa in her environment.

Space and place are in *Badlands* not the stultifying, all-encompassing places they are in *The Crying of Lot 49*.

Identity, that is, personal identity, also receives different treatment, is accorded different status, in the two countries. Rarely in the novels of the metafictionists is the writer preoccupied with the growth to maturity of a character; rarely is there a sustained interest in character unless it is a parodic character, a composite of myths and stances such as Coover's Richard Nixon or Barth's George Giles or Barthelme's Snow White. Like Humbert's construction of Lolita ("Oh, my Lolita. I have only words to play with"),[38] the metafictionists' creation of character is patent artifice, their intention being to reduce the notion of character, in and out of literature, to a false document. One has only to think of major Canadian novels of the past two decades to be convinced that a far different set of ontological values is operant. Atwood's Marian McAlpine and Mordecai Richler's Duddy Kravitz and Margaret Laurence's Hagar Shipley are far more solid characters. Their authors are engaged in writing *Bildungsromans* or other character-oriented studies; their efforts produce substantial characters who come to terms with self and world in a way that validates, either positively or negatively, their concepts of themselves and their society. Kroetsch finds the figure of the artist prominent in contemporary Canadian literature; thus, for him the *Kunstlerroman* is an oft encountered form of prose fiction. As Kroetsch pithily states, "In the beginning is the artist, beginning" (Kroetsch, p. vii). Nonetheless, the focus is perceived to be on the formation of character, whether the artist's or another's.

The growth-to-maturity novel allows for such extra-literary questions as what motivates or shapes such-and-such a character, what is his psychological set, and / or what are the sociological or philosophical inferences one can draw from a character's statements. This kind of approach would and did produce unmitigated glee in Nabokov. Ross Wetzsteon remembers Nabokov, as a teacher, referring to minor readers as those who identify with the characters. He also recalls Nabokov diagramming the themes of *Bleak House:* "He turned to the blackboard, picked up a piece of chalk, and scrawled 'the theme of inheritances' in a weird arching loop. 'The theme of generations' dipped and rose and dipped in an undulating line."[39] Wetzsteon writes that this continued until the last theme, the theme of art, was drawn, "and we suddenly realized he had drawn a cat's face, the last line its wry smile, and for the rest of the term that cat smiled out of our notebooks in mockery of the didactic approach to literature" (Wetzsteon,

p. 241). Character study also moved Gass in his essay, "The Concept of Character in Fiction," to deliver the following diatribe:

> ...characters are clearly conceived as living outside language. Just as the movie star deserts herself to put on some press agent's more alluring fictional persona, the hero of the story sets out from his own landscape for the same land of romance the star reached by stepping there from life. These people...seem to have come to the words of their novels like a visitor to town...and later they leave on the arm of the reader, bound, I suspect, for a shabbier hotel, and dubious entertainments. (*FFL*, pp. 35-36)

The whole tenor of the metafictionists' argument undermines the status of character, of identity. Such an approach is vital to Coover and it also propels even more radical, Beckett-like novels such as Rudolph Wurlitzer's *Nog* and *Flats*, which contain no hero or protagonist in the traditionally accepted sense of those words. For contemporary American writers, Michel Foucault's assessment of the self as an impending anachronism, as something that will soon be a passé historical concept, is something with which they would concur. In *Les Mots et les Choses* Foucault scorns

> all the chimeras of the new humanisms, all the facile solutions of an "anthropology" understood as a universal reflection on man, half-empirical, half-philosophical. It is comforting, however, and a source of profound relief to think that man is only a recent invention, a figure not yet two centuries old, a new wrinkle in our knowledge, and that he will disappear again as soon as that knowledge has discovered a new form.[40]

Canadian writers, on the other hand, create character as if the metafictionist and/or poststructuralist theories do not exist or at least as if they do not impinge on their own theories of fiction, specifically, and of society, generally.

The urgency and gravity of Atwood's remarks in *Survival* about the necessity of knowing here preclude the emergence of that kind of Borgesian parody of a culture that relies on the recognition that the culture parodied, despite being a creation or construct, has currency in' the minds of its citizens. Instead of the perspective winnowed from a reading of *Snow White* or *Breakfast of Champions* or *The Crying of*

Lot 49 that the culture's fictive but rigidified sense of itself should be debunked, there is in the literature and criticism of Canada the notion that the inchoate Canadian identity should be nurtured. Moreover, that identity provides reciprocal sustenance by conferring on the literati a distinctive mission, one which is peculiarly Canadian. They seek to transform what Earle Birney has called "A highschool land / deadset in adolescence"[41] into a mature nation. They see themselves as prime candidates for answering in the affirmative the question that concludes Birney's poem "Canada: Case History": "will he learn to grow up before it's too late?"[42] A glance at symposia topics, steeped in regional and national concerns, and critical studies such as W. Egglston's *The Frontier and Canadian Letters*, W. H. New's *Articulating West: Essays on Purpose and Form in Modern Canadian Literature*, Atwood's *Survival*, and John Moss's *Patterns of Isolation in English Canadian Fiction*, all of which deal with the ways winter, isolation, and the frontier affect the Canadian sensibility, reveals the Canadian men of letters' preoccupation with discussing and defining where here is and whether it is an adolescent's locale.

Interestingly, Edgar Z. Friedenberg in his forceful and lucid work, *Deference to Authority: The Case of Canada*, finds that the Canadian writer's engagement with nature is symptomatic of more than a recognition that the Canadian climate is harsh. For Friedenberg confrontations in Canadian literature have for the most part pitted man against nature because such combat is more ideologically acceptable to Canadians. Making Canadian literature an archetypal *Nanook of the North*, Friedenberg maintains the following:

> If it's Nature you're fighting, it's okay to be resourceful and competent.... It's okay to win, as Canadians clearly have — poor old Nature, poisoned unto the Arctic tundra with mercury, arsenic and asbestos wastes, has poor prospects of victory, at least in the short run. Fighting Nature doesn't make you a rebel; Nature has enormous — indeed, lethal — power, but she has no authority at all. She is entitled to no deference, which means that it is sometimes possible for Canadians to think about her honestly and with genuine awe and respect.[43]

Given the purport of Friedenberg's statements it is not surprising that *Deference to Authority* received its most laudatory review in *The New York Review of Books* and was dismissed by many Canadian reviewers as inaccurate in terms of Canadian institutions and proclivities. Despite the tendentious nature of *Deference to Authority* Friedenberg seems to me, for the most part, to be incisive about the Canadian sensibility. Nonetheless, I think that here he misapplies the deferential Canadian character. Nature's lack of authority is not the reason for its prominent appearance in Canadian fiction. Just as nature and the battle with it obsessed many nineteenth-century American novelists, Cooper, for one, it remains important because the climate and the land have not been subdued and supplanted by a strong, anthropomorphic, distinctively Canadian entity. There is not the lack of exit from Canadian culture which one sees in a work such as *Zen and the Art of Motorcycle Maintenance*. There the narrator, obeying the now clichéd dictum, "go west, young man," travels on his motorcycle from the midwest to the west coast, there to find "this hyped-up, fuck-you, supermodern, ego style of life that thinks it owns this country."[44]

Thus, it seems that there is still legitimacy in Canadian literature for the motifs of man against nature and man defining himself in the world that are treated only in an ironic or parodic manner in contemporary American literature. Regardless, just as there are British critics decrying the current lack of experimentation on the part of British novelists, there have been Canadian critics similarly exercised. George Bowering is one such writer, who argues concisely that "we can blame good old puritanism again."[45] The essay, in which he diagnoses the disease as puritanism, begins by stating, "For years I have been wondering why it is that in Canada we hold with such tenacity to realism and naturalism in our fiction" (Bowering, p. 4). Bowering then briefly cites the countries in which avant-garde fiction flourishes. Contrarily, he lists the most prominent Canadian writers "who tell the normal realist story of sensitive child growing up to be a disillusioned but wisely maladjusted adult, the most personal proof of cause and effect" (Bowering, p. 4). Bowering's assessment that the conservative character of Canadians is responsible for the retention of traditional and the disavowal of experimental methods of fiction writing finds its corollary in *Deference to Authority*.

For Friedenberg, an expatriate American whose residency in Canada began in 1970 and whose book was written at the end of that decade, Canadian and American sensibilities are most sharply differentiated in Canadians' conservatism which manifests itself as deference to authority. A dichotomy along these lines also produced Wallace Stegner's definition of Canadians as predisposed to law and order, and Americans to lawlessness.[46] Friedenberg maintains that

California's vitality, "recognized throughout the world as unmistakable in its variety, vulgarity and vigor," contrasts sharply with a Canadian aura that "is substantially colorless, odorless, noninfectious and nonoffensive."[47] The arts in Canada, he claims, have suffered as a result. Friedenberg identifies ballet as the art form in which Canada has achieved international recognition. For him ballet is the artistic medium which provides the most minimal opportunity for spontaneity or improvisation; he regards it as a medium which is inherently conservative. Conservatism is also acknowledged as an intrinsic part of the Canadian character by Beverly Rasporich who maintains that it is at the heart of Stephen Leacock's humour; Rasporich differentiates that humour from American humour because of the nervousness embedded in the latter: "the real persona of Leacock's humour [is] that of the educated Anglo-Saxon gentleman. With his sure values of dignified living, his books, his club, his civilized comforts, he was the author's instructive response to his own quickly developing industrial society and to North American society at large."[48]

Another Canadian who writes receptively of the avant-garde, interestingly enough in this case in the vocabulary of the postmodernist artist and critic, is Kroetsch who speaks of "foregrounding" language and "deconstructing" conventions. Kroetsch was for a time co-editor and is presently an associate editor for poetry and fiction of *boundary 2: A Journal of Postmodern Literature*. His sense of the metafictive is apt and incisive, and his own fiction has its radical engagement with traditional forms. In a paper delivered at the Modern Language Association Convention in 1980 Kroetsch touches on an interesting issue tangential to the one developed in this study. That paper, "For Play and Entrance: The Contemporary Canadian Long Poem," makes the case for the experimental character of the long Canadian poem:

> Delay, in the contemporary long poem (that necessary resisting towards the condition of art), has devolved upon the language itself, instead of into new resources of narrative. The language has become so foregrounded that the dialectic with narrative very nearly fails. Or else: the narrative, adhering to old grammars, refuses the excitement of its own language.[49]

Poetry, of course, has a tradition in which narrative and language are not simply connected; this is not the case in the history of the novel. Therefore, it is not anomalous to confront the poems that Kroetsch lists in a long bibliography appended to his paper. The peculiar conditions of fiction make it an interesting phenomenon to observe insofar as a comparison of Canadian and American practices are concerned. That the divergent practices in fiction are not reflected in poetry is due largely to poetic tradition and theory rather than to the idiosyncratic qualities in the sensibilities of the two countries.

Not only have there occasionally been critics who have encouraged what Bowering calls a more epistemological direction for Canadian fiction, but there have also been those critics who have assailed the dominant critical tradition itself for much of the conservatism of Canadian fiction. Most notably, Canadian critics were chastized in the mid-seventies for being bad readers in the Nabokovian sense of the term. Such an assault is contained in Frank Davey's article "Surviving the Paraphrase." Davey cites an obsession with thematic criticism, with sociological criticism, with the kind of criticism that emphasizes cultural and devalues structural concerns. "The movement here is towards paraphrase — paraphrase of the culture and paraphrase of the literature. The critic extracts for his deliberations the paraphrasable content and throws away the form. He attends to the explicit meaning of the work and neglects whatever content is implicit in its structure, language...."[50] Moreover, whenever structure and language are examined, they are handled with the biases of the school of new criticism. Seldom does one find the non-mimetic, anti-referential perspectives on the medium of prose fiction which are presented in journals such as *New Literary History* and *Diacritics* or in the critical writings of Edward Said, René Girard or those such as Geoffrey Hartman, J. Hillis Miller, Harold Bloom, and Paul de Man, who are often referred to as the Yale Deconstructionists. Derrida's persistent attack on the Western metaphysical tradition generally and on the teleological dimensions of the language of fiction specifically has been adapted by many American scholars possibly because of the feisty quality of literary criticism in the United States, possibly because the glut of Ph.D.s in the humanities has caused those driven to publish to seek new entrées into literature, but probably because in the tenets of poststructuralism they discover the philosophy of metafiction. For Derrida "to be is to-be-in-the-book,"[51] to be enmeshed in the "necessary *exchange* of one's existence with or for the letter" (Derrida, p.70). At his pithiest he writes, "In the beginning is hermeneutics" (Derrida, p.67). Such a congruence, found in the devaluation of the transparency of language, and in the ineluctable engagement with language, is absent in the Canadian context in which the staples of traditional fiction still are accorded legitimate status. Davey has, it should be mentioned, provided a forum for avant-garde literature and criticism in *Open Letter*, a journal he edits. The Winter 1980-81 issue of *Open Letter*, for instance, contains a playful, Derridean section devoted to Canadian genealogy called "Towards a Grammatology of the Canadian Unconscious," which meticulously reports in deadpan manner the discovery of the Piccu Carlu pyramid and other ruins in Southern Ontario. Such whimsy, however, appears to be alien to works and issues in the foreground of Canadian culture and can be read as a satiric comment on more mainstream concerns.

A survey of recent Canadian criticism reveals the absence of what has become a vitriolic debate in the United States pitting the forces of tradition against the forces of deconstruction; that debate even found its way into *Time* magazine, a sure sign that it has achieved notoriety. Frye, when interviewed about the publication of his book on the Bible, *The Great Code: The Bible and Literature*, admitted his interest in the theories of Derrida and his acolytes. However, he has not been moved to answer or engage those theories even though, as Frank Lentricchia points out in *After the New Criticism*, they challenge the fixed schema and ahistoricity which are essential to the arguments developed in *Anatomy of Criticism: Four Essays*. Nor have many other Canadian critics moved to participate in the debate between Derrideans and their detractors, the whole issue seemingly being so remote from their enterprises. Little which engages contemporary critical theory has been produced. An essay such as "Word and Fact: Laurence and the Problem of Language"[52] by Theo Quayle Dombrowski eddies around Derrida's notion of a labyrinthine, self-reflective, non-referential language and Roland Barthes's contention that the language of prose fiction is a closed system, a semiotical play-field; however, these theoreticians are neither cited nor acknowledged. The writer accepts the now challenged premise that the language of fiction is, in Ortega y Gasset's metaphor, a window onto the world instead of writing *on* the window which retards mimetic and referential entrées. Similarly, "The Fabular Fiction of Robert Kroetsch"[53] by P. L. Surette alludes in a footnote to *The Fabulators*, but does not place *Gone Indian* in the framework of the new historical fiction, works such as *The Public Burning* or *The Sot-Weed Factor* in which historical personages appear and have their attitudes, opinions, and sensibilities depicted as being stylized and artificial. Ondaatje's method in *The Collected Works of Billy the Kid*, his deconstruction of history, is, as has been stated, akin to the method of the metafictionists. However, Dennis Lee in *Savage Fields: An Essay in Literature and Cosmology* assesses the work's scope on a more generalized plane: "The form of *Billy the Kid* is affected by its cosmological intuition."[54] Nabokov's injunction that cosmic is always in danger of losing its "s" is apposite here. There are, perhaps, signs that critical isolationism in Canada is being mitigated somewhat. A recent essay by Barbara Godard in *Essays on Canadian Writing*, called "My (m)Other, My Self: Strategies for Subversion in Atwood and Hébert," seeks to make the poststructuralist case that confrontation with a patriarchal or sexist society can emerge not only in a direct way but also in an oxymoronic or parodic way.[55] For Godard *Lady Oracle* is a self-reflexive novel, one with a narrative that is *mise en abîme*, one that is complete with distorting mirrors and narratives within narratives.

In the special Summer 1977 issue of *Studies in Canadian Literature*, entitled "Minus Canadian," Barry Cameron and Michael Dixon attempt to confront what they regard as the two shibboleths adumbrated in the preceding paragraphs. Their first objective is to evaluate the stereotypical assessment of Canadian literature: "The entire phenomenon consists simply of theme — and a singular theme at that, 'survival in a garrison' — having only two connotations: sociological and/or autobiographical."[56] This, they feel, contains a pernicious misreading of Canadian literature; for them the country's fiction is replete with formal devices, with structural nuances and sophistication, making the novels something other than loose, diffuse narratives held together by nothing other than plot and/or hero. Cameron and Dixon argue that because the novels in their purview combine complex image patterns and symbolic structures, because they reward the scrupulous textural forays of the school of new (now rather dated) criticism, they qualify as part of what Frye calls the autonomous world of literature; that is, they can profitably be studied within the parameters of textual analysis rather than as part of the Canadian identity or the Canadian experience or another such extra-literary context. While Cameron's and Dixon's debunking of the notion of a narrowly parochial focus in Canadian fiction is argued convincingly enough, their scope is admittedly modest. The essays in their journal do not, they say, "propound some startling, new philosophy of literary criticism. This sort of attention and respect has been accorded works from other literatures for decades."[57] In other words, one should not go to "Minus Canadian" to find unearthed the radical breaks with traditional fiction that are outlined in Robbe-Grillet's manifesto, *Pour Un*

Nouveau Roman, or in Gass's devaluation of realistic fiction in *Fiction and the Figures of Life* and *The World within The Word* or in Nabokov's brilliant, Wildean aperçus on anti-mimetic literature ("Literature does not tell the truth but it makes it up..." [Wetzsteon, p.242]). Nor are Cameron and Dixon interested in literature which challenges the supposed verities of the novel: John Hawkes might contend that the true enemies of the novel are plot, character, theme, and setting, but Cameron and Dixon chide Davey for his post-modernist bias in *From There to Here: A Guide to English-Canadian Literature since 1960*. What Cameron and Dixon are interested in exploring are the structural devices that reveal the artistry of traditional novels written in Canada.

The second objective in "Minus Canadian" is to rectify the critical wrongs spawned by parochial considerations and nationally oriented critical approaches. That Cameron and Dixon assess Canadian criticism as being in a disadvantaged condition is noteworthy; however, here again their scope is limited. The object of their wrath is not the school of new criticism but rather nationalistic criticism. Inveighing against the sociological approach to literature, they enunciate critical precepts that reflect the autonomy of a work of art. Stridently they assert the following: "That we must state such self-evident canons of responsible criticism, and feel compelled to defend them in an atmosphere of polemical homily, is of course ludicrous — an embarrassing symptom of the immature state of commentary on Canadian literature."[58]

John Moss, in "Bushed in the Sacred Wood," a piece collected in the second series of David Helwig's *The Human Elements*, makes a like-minded call for the movement away from a nationalistic focus. His essay contains an extensive catalogue of thematic criticisms, an orthodoxy he feels it is time to debunk. In *Essays on Canadian Writing*, No. 11, Russell M. Brown also advocates a redefinition of Canadian criticism. His essay, "Critic, Culture, Text: Beyond Thematics," as the title indicates, espies the identical enemy. Despite these demands for revision (the act of seeing again) and despite the declamatory statements of Davey, Dixon, and Cameron as well as the measured criticism of Bowering, the anorectic Canadian identity and its concomitant critical nurturing, which are primarily responsible for traditional fiction and criticism, do not appear to be altering radically or even evolving into other forms. What W. H. New wrote in the mid-seventies at the beginning of his essay on Canada in *Among Worlds: An Introduction to Modern Commonwealth and South African Fiction* seems still to prevail: "Searching for the national identity is a kind of congenital art form in Canada, which has provided both the theme for many poets and novelists and the substance of much critical observation and expectation."[59] Certainly if *Canadian Literature in the 70's* is any indication, that predilection among critics and novelists for writing about a Canadian identity works deleteriously on Canadian literature. Of all Robertson Davies' works it is "The Canada of Myth and Reality," a clichéd and jingoistic essay on nationalism, that was chosen by editors Edwards and Denham. The strain of creating an identity dominates the tone of Davies' hortatory piece:

> ...it is in poetry and fiction that the questers repose their greatest hopes. A Canadian literature, recognizable as such at home and abroad, is what they want. But the creation of a national literature is almost as slow as the building of a coral atoll; toil as we may, the recognizable island will not rise above the waves in a very great hurry. But we are working at it, and we have made rather more progress than some of our more anxious Canadian watchers seem to understand.[60]

Davies' royal "we," his hope for a seamless body of literature that would voice unmistakably Canadian virtues, indeed the tone of the whole piece — all contrast markedly with the direction taken by American authors, who hardly see themselves as creating a reified identity of any kind. They regard their country as too enamoured of its identity and wish to deflate it. Again here the cathectic American, anorectic Canadian motif presents itself quite acutely.

The Canadian critics' fixation on nationalism is understandable given the context I have tried to develop, and considering the Social Sciences and Humanities Research Council guidelines (which, after all, promise remuneration for patriotic forays into criticism). Understandable, too, is the Canadian fiction writers' preoccupation with the theme, although the reasons for this preoccupation are more paradoxical. In a short essay in *Books in Canada*, Roch Carrier provides a witty insight into the fate of the writers whose separatist visions have become ensconced, institutionalized, in the Parti Québécois' assumption of power. They have, he tells us, become peripheral to the ideological thrusting of an inchoate but compelling national identity. Carrier mentions that one writer, who clamoured for the implementation of PQ programs, can be found "buying the blue shirts his Cabinet minister will wear on television."[61] The majority of the pre-empted but comfortably co-opted writer-prophets can also be found "in one of the fashionable restaurants: they've all put on weight since the PQ came to power" (Carrier, p. 14). Those whose perspectives don't exactly coincide with PQ positions are also silenced, "stifled by guilt, or they choose to put off the act of writing till later, telling themselves they must do nothing against the PQ before it's been given a chance..." (Carrier, p. 15). Carrier, in short, taunts his confrères with the knowledge that, as his title indicates, the party is the pen, that the party stamps its ideological configurations on the province and that beside this monolith the writer is insignificant.

National identities are inflated constructs, products of advertising and politics. The uproar that Davies writes about in "The Canada of Myth and Reality" ("at present the uproar is for a Canadian identity")[62] is one which is not primarily of the artist's making. That he succumbs to an obsession with it consigns him, as Carrier discerns in the Québécois writer's situation, to irrelevance; it dispossesses him because there are agencies with far greater powers than writers of fiction have to package and label the identity and profit by its manifestations. Davies' notions that Canadians are in a position to afford a new cultural suit presumes that they should go to the Canadian artist for a fitting; it implies both a presumption about and a prescription for the nature of the artist. Carrier's essay, "The Party Is the Pen," consigns the construction of a public and viable identity to more willing if much less trustworthy and imaginative creators; his artist is too idiosyncratic, too subversive for such a function. Most English Canadian writers, it should be noted, do not subscribe to the programmatic growth of an identifiably Canadian literature, except insofar as that literature is a diverse body of work identifiable as Canadian only by virtue of the fact that it was written by those who were born in and/or live in Canada. Nonetheless, there is on the part of Davies, Horwood, and Atwood, among others, the occasional hagiographic attempt to nurture their country in their literature. As will be seen graphically in the following chapter such an attempt in the United States is anathema to Gass and the other metafictionists. About the relationship of the artist and society Gass writes,

> Naturally the artist is an enemy of the state. He cannot play politics, succumb to slogans and other simplifications, worship heroes, ally himself with any party, suck on some politician's program like a sweet.... *He undermines everything*. Even when, convinced of the rightness of a cause, he

30

dedicates his skills to a movement, he cannot simplify, he cannot overlook, he cannot forget, omit, or falsify. In the end the movement must reject or even destroy him. (*FFL*, pp. 287-88; emphasis added)

As for future directions, Barthelme's wry and legitimate prediction is that his own style of writing will flourish until some other mode, just as good, supplants it with different formulae, different values; there will be, as there has always been, a new aesthetic to replace the old. This insight seems to me to be germane vis-à-vis the situations in both countries. In the United States the last ten years have provided some backlash against metafiction. Saul Bellow's remarks about the apparent demise of social realism and books such as Gardner's *On Moral Fiction* and Mary McCarthy's *Ideas and the Novel*, which attack the virtuosity and legerdemain of the metafictionists as being sterile and solipsistic, have had their supporters. To quote one of them, Charles Molesworth, "to choose between, say, John Barth and S. Beckett, might be to choose between two exhaustions, two forms of fully articulated 'belatedness.' As we used to say back home, 'mighty slim pickens,' indeed."[63] Nonetheless, Barth, Barthelme, Coover, and the other writers of metafiction are young enough that given the ambitious scope of many of their recent works (Barth's *Letters*, Coover's *The Public Burning*, and William Gaddis' *JR*) they will most probably continue to experiment with the parameters of prose fiction. Also, the *Fiction Collective* which publishes novels regarded as not viable commercially will likely continue to publish works in a similar vein by lesser known writers. Noteworthy, too, is the ease with which Barthelme accepts the inevitable displacement of his mode of writing by another.

Although Kroetsch can be seen to be a transitional figure who is alert and receptive to the deconstructive quality of contemporary American literature and although there are many writers such as Martin Myers, Jack Hodgins, Robert Allen, Audrey Thomas, David Young, and Ray Smith who have metafictive leanings, the dominant direction of Canadian literature will continue, it seems, along more traditional lines. Although this need not and in all probability will not produce a stagnant literature, there are in Canada as there are in the United States those who resist their literature's prevailing tendencies. Of *Aurora!*, *New Canadian Writing 1980* reviewer Carole Corbeil writes, "The greater number of the stories in *Aurora!* are naturalistic, and the naturalistic these days is only immediately compelling if the voice behind them is compelling."[64] Corbeil states further that *Aurora!* disappoints and does so because the writers collected there do not take risks. The collection includes, in fact, a dialogue between Frye and Robert Fulford that eddies around the notion that cultural maturity is defined in terms of regionalism. It indicates that the obsession with the development of a Canadian identity has by no means run its course.

If Americans are emblazoned in Canadians' minds and in many of their own minds as Coover's rapacious Uncle Sam and Canadians are ensconced in American as well as their own minds as the bland Bob and Doug McKenzie of Second City TV's Great White North, it probably affirms Oscar Wilde's maxim, "life imitates art." It also attests to the tendency of both national and personal lives to become fixed and clichéd. Kroetsch, yoking Canadian and American literary enterprises, has written, "A reading of the world is at best a misreading of the world" (Kroetsch, p. ix). Nonetheless, that reading often tends to gain legitimacy. Propagated in the literature and culture of Canada and the United States are the notions of a cathectic America and an anorectic Canada. Metafiction, an essential weapon of deconstruction, flourishes in the United States to combat the American monolith. On the other hand, metafiction, undercutting as it does thematic meaning and ontological certitude, is not conducive to nurturing what is thought to be a malnourished Canadian identity.

America: Gass and Coover

"This is the country of brain damage."
— Barthelme, "Brain Damage"

IT IS NOT HARD to cull from contemporary American fiction passages that attack America, specifically, or constituted identities, generally. Examples abound: strident, flippant, ironic, parodic ones. Ken Kesey's assaults are wrathful, Vladimir Nabokov's bemused, Thomas Pynchon's abstruse, Kurt Vonnegut's deliberately naive. The target in each case, though, is as explicit as it is in Allen Ginsberg's "America." The country's seeming richness and diversity are reduced to America's inspissated icons and ideology. The flag, the national anthem, the Statue of Liberty, the dollar bill — all are copied onto the pages of *Breakfast of Champions*, then held up to ridicule. Despite the convoluted dimensions of *The Crying of Lot 49*, Oedipa's forays are undertaken explicitly to supplant the staples of American life, Tupperware parties and muzak ("the Fort Wayne Settecento Ensemble's variorum recording of the Vivaldi Kazoo Concerto, Boyd Beaver, soloist");[1] she yearns to find what Pynchon calls "pulsing stelliferous Meaning"[2] that will transform her mundane circumstances. To accept mainstream American life is to lead an attenuated, sterile existence is the novel's premise. The Tristero system, a real or imagined labyrinth, in which she becomes enmeshed, offers the only outlet, in contrast to the United States Postal Service, here a metaphor for bland, conventional communication:

> Either you have stumbled indeed, without the aid of LSD or other indole alkaloids, onto a secret richness and concealed density of dream; onto a network by which x number of Americans are truly communicating whilst reserving their lies, recitations of routine, arid betrayals of spiritual poverty, for the official government delivery system; maybe even onto a real alternative to the exitlessness, to the absence of surprise to life, that harrows the head of everybody American you know, and you too, sweetie.[3]

In *One Flew Over the Cuckoo's Nest* the denizens of America are similarly straitjacketed. There the American dream has turned into the Combine, love it or leave it. Those who do not function smoothly in and for the machine, in other words, the blacks, Indians, and rabbits, the sensitive ones, are destroyed or removed to an institution, the ward, for retooling. "Yes. This is what I know. The ward is a factory for the Combine."[4] Despite Chief Bromden's paranoid notions about electrodes, wires, transmitters, and so on being planted everywhere and in everything, Kesey's metaphor is meant with immediacy and fervency — "But it's the truth even if it didn't happen."[5] The cuckoo's nest that is America is only evaded, if it is escaped at all, not confronted or overthrown. As with Kesey, himself, and his Merry Pranksters in their ingestion of drugs and their defiance of social norms, lives celebrated, of course, in Tom Wolfe's *The Electric Kool-Aid Acid Test*, the characters in *One Flew Over the Cuckoo's Nest* regard the monolith as besieging and imprisoning them.

More playfully developed is the view of American life which Nabokov works into *Lolita*. Conventional Mrs. Haze (later Mrs. Humbert) and Lolita — Nabokov reveals amidst the legerdemain, the puns, anagrams, and literary allusions that are at the heart of the novel, how clichéd these people are. They represent those who live in stylized houses modelled after *Your Home Is You*. With the "authoress" of this book "[Mrs. Haze] developed a hatred for little lean chairs and spindle tables" (Nabokov, p. 73). Their stylized mores and manners are shaped by *A Guide to Your Child's Development*, The Beardsley Star's "Column for Teens," and the Ramsdale *Journal*'s "Society Column," as well as by "soap operas, psychoanalysis and cheap novelettes." Concerning Mrs. Humbert's appetite for stories about Humbert's continental and cosmopolitan past, "the more popular and platitudinous" Humbert made them, "the more Mrs. Humbert was pleased with the show" (Nabokov, p. 75). *Lolita* not only gently mocks stylized living, but it also parodies stylized writing; it contains vignettes which ape thrillers, soap operas, cheap novelettes, and the lingos of psychoanalysis and learned journals among many other kinds of writing. Nabokov finds "muddle crass" or middle class American life very amusing.

The pithiest fictions, which vitiate received as opposed to created ways of living in America, are Donald Barthelme's. With phrases, mannerisms, values, and objects that are *de rigueur*, Barthelme's characters consistently divulge themselves as patent artifice. "Critique de la Vie Quotidienne," one of Barthelme's best stories, chronicles the entwined lives of a separated couple: "Perhaps we are part of a trend,"[6] the husband says. In *Elle* the wife reads so many *actualité* pieces devoted to Anna Karina, the movie star, that, we are told wryly, she begins to resemble her; the husband is fatherly and alcoholic in appropriate proportions. Fashionable wines, food, and utensils also define them. Their separation removes them to equally stereotyped places and patterns:

> Wanda is happier now, I think. She has taken herself off to Nanterre, where she is studying Marxist sociology with Lefebvre.... The child is being cared for in an experimental nursery school for the children of graduate students run, I understand, in accord with the best Piagetian principles. And I, I have my J & B.[7]

In "The Great Debate," a proleptic transcription of the Gerald Ford-Jimmy Carter Presidential debate of 1976, Carter and Ford speak in the caricatured ways by which they had come to be known. "Carter: He that hath Love in his heart hath in his heart Love.... Ford: ...I didn't call it that, Secretary Kissinger called it that, and because he called it that I just naturally, as who wouldn't, began calling it that."[8] Clichéd fathers addressing their sons in clichéd ways in *The Dead Father* ("Hey son. Hey boy. Let's you and me go out and throw the ball around. Throw the ball around.");[9] self-consciously alienated moderns seeking to solve their modern dilemmas in *Snow White* ("We suffer today I believe from a lack of connection with each other. That is common knowledge, so common in fact, that it may not even be true.")[10] — over and over again Barthelme's wit focusses on mannered thinking, living, being.

John Barth, Max Apple, Richard Brautigan, and Don DeLillo are just a few other writers who immediately come to mind as having produced fictions which seek to deflate or otherwise engage the American identity and its stylized manifestations. Clearly, the perception of contemporary American writers is that an ideology has inflated and distorted American activities; correspondingly, these writers seek to reduce the potency of such an ideology, to demystify or, in Roland Barthes's terms, demythify it. Barthes, especially as the writer of *Mythologies*, is an apt model here. In *Mythologies* Barthes operates on many facets of French life — wrestling, vacationing, detergents, the popular conception of the artist, and so on — in order to denaturalize them, to read them and reveal them as signs and to discover their loaded dimensions.

The whole of France is steeped in this anonymous ideology: our press, our films, our theatre, our pulp literature, our rituals, our Justice, our diplomacy, our conversations, our remarks about the weather, a murder trial, a touching wedding, the cooking we dream of, the garments we wear, everything in every day life is dependent on the representation which the bourgeoisie *has and makes us have* of the relations between men and the world.[11]

The writer of metafiction is a semiologist in much the same way Barthes is. He reveals that all elements of American life, the trivial as well as the portentous, are caught in a system of signs; they are never spontaneous or innocent. A. B. Paulson, for instance, writes a parody of the Minnesota Multiphasic Personality Inventory, which he called "The Minnesota Multiphasic Personality: a diagnostic test in two parts." The reader of the story is invited to place his name and other information in the appropriate boxes, then to answer MMPI-like questions. It is only perhaps when he reaches Section B, question number 8, "T F I have not made lewd faces at matrons descending escalators,"[12] that the reader recognizes Paulson's technique of starting him with a more or less legitimate context then moving him and the test further and further towards the arbitrary and the ludicrous. The verifiability of the personality or vocational profile that emerges from such a test is probably undermined ever after.

In *Edwin Mullhouse: The Life and Death of an American Writer, 1943–54 by Jeffrey Cartwright*, Steven Millhauser authors his author, Cartwright, in a manner akin to Nabokov's authoring of Humbert Humbert. In the process Millhauser produces a witty parody of biography, having Cartwright divide his book, which chronicles the eleven years Mullhouse lived, into the early years, the middle years, and the late years. Comedy results from the transformation of Mullhouse into the person Cartwright wishes him to be despite the former's struggles against being so shaped. Biographer ordering a life, providing a schema for his subject, giving fixity to inchoate life—these are the mechanical biographer's steps that Millhauser parodies. One further example of seemingly unconnected and natural dimensions of life that American writers act upon as semiologists is Alan Goldfein's treatment of philosophers as fiction-makers in *Heads: A Metafictional History of Western Civilization, 1762–1975*. Goldfein situates many of the world's greatest philosophers in worlds of their own making, most memorably portraying Jean-Paul Sartre as a boxing manager who continually yells "Persistence precedes *presence*"[13] at his beleaguered protégé.

One could assemble American mythologies as numerous as those French ones Barthes examines. What is clear is that no aspect of American life, religious, philosophical, economic, social, literary, is permitted to retain its reality, its ontological security. The writers I have cited would probably concur with Barthes, who writes in his preface to *Mythologies*, "The starting point of these reflections was usually a feeling of impatience at the sight of the 'naturalness' with which newspapers, art and common sense constantly dress up a reality which, even though it is the one we live in, is undoubtedly determined by history" (Barthes, p. 11). Of course, what exercises contemporary American writers most is the naturalness of the American character and the American state. The latter is, in Vonnegut's terminology, a "granfalloon," an arbitrary unit that achieves reified status and that elicits devotion and false bonding from its members.

There are many writers whose work one could legitimately claim to be representative in terms delimited by my initial chapter. There are many writers who both experiment with the form of fiction and confront the American identity; many, similarly, regard constituted identities of all kinds as fictions. John Hawkes's famous maxim, cited in the previous chapter, is that the true enemies of the novel are plot, character, theme, and setting; Barth, one can be reminded again, has whimsically written that "God wasn't a bad novelist, but he was a realist," inferring that writers of his ilk find the conventions of art and life jejune. Both Barth and Hawkes have received a great deal of critical attention with many books, articles, dissertations, and symposia having been devoted to their fiction. Other major writers of metafiction such as Barthelme and Pynchon have had their work subjected to an inordinate amount of critical scrutiny. Pynchon's novels, especially, because of their recondite scientific motifs, have been studied extensively and also idiosyncratically in journals which rarely treat fiction. Nonetheless, it is not merely to provide a different perspective on metafiction and its relationship to America that I am focussing attention in this chapter on Gass and Coover. Both, in these years of frantic scholarly output, especially where contemporary American fiction is concerned, have received less extensive and more tepid commentary than their confrères. Coover, though, is the object of a study by Richard Anderson in the Twayne United States Authors Series and

Gass was for a time the flagship writer on fiction for *The New York Review of Books*, producing essays that have been collected in *Fiction and the Figures of Life* and *The World within the Word*.

More pertinent, though, than their relative neglect by critics is their seminal place in contemporary American letters and especially in the context of this book. It is Gass, after all, who coined the term metafiction: "the forms of fiction serve as the material upon which further forms can be imposed. Indeed, many of the so-called anti-novels are really metafictions."[14] Also, it is Gass whose insightful, witty, and incisive essays make up the theoretical framework for metafiction. In the essay "The Last Quixote: Marginal Notes on the Gospel According to Samuel Beckett" and in the stories which make up *Pricksongs and Descants*, Coover engages similar theoretical concerns. However, it is his novels, most notably *The Public Burning*, which provide a vivid object-lesson in the potency of metafiction and its confrontation with the American identity. It is, then, because their work challenges with unparalleled flair and trenchant combativeness cathectic America, and its social and artistic dimensions, that Gass and Coover are examined in the following pages.

"The ladies egged him on; in Eve's name, they dared him; so he made love with discreet verbs and light nouns, delicate conjunctions."[15] The situation is that of Jethro Furber, protagonist of *Omensetter's Luck*, Gass's only published novel to date. However, it introduces William Gass as aptly as can be done. Gass's logodaedaly, the world he creates within his words, is genuinely awesome. Ihab Hassan has written of Gass's dexterity with language as follows: "Gass remains a writer born, made and self-remade, who can write sentences, by the hundreds, that would tempt Torquemada to forgive for each word a heretic at the stake."[16] His output has, to be sure, been modest: two collections of essays, *Fiction and the Figures of Life* and *The World within the Word*, and a novel, *Omensetter's Luck*, as well as a collection of short stories, *In the Heart of the Heart of the Country*, a novella, *Willie Master's Lonesome Wife*, a philosophical tour-de-force, *On Being Blue: A Philosophical Inquiry*, and excerpts from *The Tunnel*, a yet to be released novel, which seems intermittently to collapse. Gass, in the theory and practice of literature, has produced an uncompromisingly innovative and dexterous oeuvre that is bitter ("Even as a grown man I was still desperately boasting that I'd choose another cunt to come from");[17] lyrical ("And shall this reader, as you

38

open the book, shadow the page like a palm? perhaps (mind the strain on the eyes); and sink into the paper? become the print?" [Gass, Preface, p. xlvi]); and iconoclastic ("Hamlet has his history in the heart, and none of us will ever be as real, as vital, as complex and living as he is — a total creature of the stage" [FFL, p. 283]). Vilified by John Gardner in *On Moral Fiction* and by Gerald Graff in *Literature against Itself* for violating the norms of fiction, Gass does so with such irreverence, panache, and verve that the arguments against Gass's percepts, especially in *On Moral Fiction*, couched as they are in pedestrian prose, reveal nothing but their shop-worn, conventional nature.

The Preface to the most recent edition of *In the Heart of the Heart of the Country* contains a good introduction to Gass's subversive aesthetic, his insight into the language of fiction. Gass writes,

> I am fashioning a reader for these fictions...of what kind? well, skilled and generous with attention, for one thing, patient with longeurs, forgiving of every error and indulgence, avid for details...ah, and a lover of lists, a twiddler of lines. Shall this reader be given occasionally to mouthing a word aloud or wanting to read to a companion in a piercing library whisper? yes; and shall this reader be one whose breathing changes with the tenses of the verbs? yes;...but we won't need hair or nose or any other opening or lure...not a muscle need be imagined...a body indifferent to time, to diet...what? oh, a sort of slowpoke singer, finger tracer, then, mover of lips....(Preface, p. xlv)

Radiating through these words, this portrait, is the Nabokov, remembered by Wetzsteon, who when teaching his course on modern literature would tell students there were two million words on the course, actually one million in the books, which were to be read twice, the first time to get rid of such trivial concerns as plot suspense; the Nabokov who said "Caress the details," meaning the language, not the eponymous little girl of *Lolita*; the Nabokov whose maxim it is that "the first literature is the boy crying wolf"; and finally the Nabokov who referred to minor readers as those who identified with the characters in novels.[18] Over and over again Gass sustains his own assault on the shibboleths that irked Nabokov. In "Philosophy and the Form of Ficton" he maintains that "the novelist, if he is any good, will keep us kindly imprisoned in his language — there is literally nothing beyond"

(*FFL*, p.8). Also, in "Gertrude Stein: Her Escape from Protective Language" he indicts both conventional criticism, "which has lived like a shrew upon paraphrase and explanation" (*FFL*, p.92), and the traditional novel which employs language "like the gray inaudible wife who services the great man: an ideal engine, utterly self-effacing, devoted without remainder to its task" (*FFL*, p.93).

Later, it will be seen that such quotidian deployment of language shapes and ensnares identities both individual and collective. For now, however, it is worthwhile to remain with Gass and his notions of the language of fiction; this is so because the ramifications of such an aesthetic extend beyond mere showing off, the accusation levelled by Gardner. There have, of course, been doctrines formulated, especially since Henry James's "The Art of Fiction," and other of his essays and prefaces, that have demanded of novelists that they write other than diffuse, plot-oriented novels ("loose, baggy monsters" was, I think, James's phrase for them). Virginia Woolf, for instance, labelled novelists whose focus was external materialists. Gustave Flaubert's maxim was that "the finest works are those that contain the least matter."[19] André Gide contended: "Outward events, accidents, traumatisms, belong to the cinema. The novel should leave them to it."[20] Nonetheless, although the practitioners of the early modern novel eschewed external realism, by and large for an internal realism, their confrontation with the traditional limits of the genre did not terminate irrefutably the debate. In a humorous and inimitable tirade, Gass carries on the argument against tradition:

> For most people, fiction is history; fiction is history without tables, graphs, dates, imports, edicts, evidence, laws; history without hiatus — intelligible, simple, smooth. Fiction is sociology freed of statistics, politics with no real party in the opposition; it's a world where play money buys you cardboard squares of colored country; a world where everyone is obediently psychological, economic, ethnic, geographical — framed in a keyhole and always nude, each figure fashioned from the latest thing in cello-see-through, so we may observe our hero's guts, too, if we choose: ah, they're blue, and squirming like a tickled river. For truth without effort, thought without rigor, feeling without form, existence without commitment: what will you give? for a wind-up world, a toy life? ... six bits? for a book with a thicker skin? ... six bucks? I am a man, myself, intemperately mild, and though it seems to me as much

deserved as it's desired, I have no wish to steeple quires of paper passion up so many sad unelevating rears. (*FFL*, p. 30)

For too long, claim Gass and the other writers of metafiction, novelists have been lazily content to accept the easy intercourse between fiction and reality, "to people a world where play money buys you cardboard squares of colored country." Their orientation has been mimetic; they have induced the reader to wander in social and economic realms, encouraged him to shift indiscriminately from novelist's world to reality. Moreover, they have posited the easy interchange between language and reality. A concomitant diatribe of Gass's is presented in his essay "The Concept of Character in Fiction." If the language of fiction is perceived to be transparent, then characters are regarded as the *sine qua non* of fiction; furthermore, they "are clearly conceived as living outside language" (*FFL*, p. 35). Novel as tapestry, as construct — this is, for Gass, fiction's realm: "There are no descriptions in fiction, there are only constructions, and the principles which govern these constructions are persistently philosophical" (*FFL*, p. 17).

Just as the battle with the reified American identity pervades all dimensions of society, the battle with the reified novel engages all dimensions of the genre. Currently, the battle is especially acute insofar as the relationship of language to experience and to world is concerned. Is language a neutral conduit, an instrument or medium that explains world or do the two not coexist in such classical and comfortable ways? Michel Foucault writes that discourse "is not a slender surface of contact, or confrontation, between a reality and a language, the intrication of the lexicon and an experience."[21] For Foucault, man is enmeshed in a language which cannot conduct him to some supra-linguistic realm where truth flourishes and world is explained by words. Gass is clearly of this camp, of the movement that denies easy passage from signifier to signified. Language for him, as for Foucault, replicates itself, fractures itself, and is self-reflexive. Indeed, not only his theoretical statements about the dimensions of fiction, but also the scope of his own fiction encompasses the relationship of language and world. Like Nabokov's Humbert Humbert in *Lolita*, Hawkes's Cyril in *The Blood Oranges*, Coover's J. Henry Waugh in *The Universal Baseball Association, Inc.: J. Henry Waugh, Prop.*, and Barthelme's Snow White in *Snow White*, Gass's narrators contend with the contradiction inherent in the shaping powers of language and the resistant, inchoate matter of reality. They recognize the irreconcilable gap between those two disparate entities.

41

One such narrator is Furber of *Omensetter's Luck*. He is one of three monologuists, each of whom tries to tell the story of Omensetter. Their fictions are so idiosyncratic that only the natural, accepting Omensetter penetrates the localized perspectives. Israbestis Tott's section is replete with stories ("I call that story the story of Kick's cat's fierce revenge, or sometimes I call it the story of the boys who played at bandits" [*OL*, p. 27]) or rather incomplete stories; ironically, the story he wants to tell about Omensetter is barely begun. Henry Pimber's monologue eddies around Omensetter's unconscious acceptance of life; unable to shake his own modern consciousness, Pimber commits suicide. And finally there is Furber whose *"beautiful barriers of words"* constitute a magnificent but insane failure to tell the story that would outdo Omensetter's placid assurance. At one point in his incessant monologue which constitutes the bulk of the novel, Furber inwardly sings:

> My lips are highly rated,
> and my fingers celebrated,
> as for my tongue, it's equally fun,
> however it's rotated...

(OL, p. 146)

A reading of "The Reverend Jethro Furber's Change of Heart" confirms that Furber's tongue is rotated in many different ways. Yet all the riddles, rhymes, and puns that Furber concocts cannot take him close to *logos*. They cannot even conduct him to the peace of mind and tranquillity which it is Brackett Omensetter's luck to possess. The main thrust of *Omensetter's Luck* resides in Furber's attempts, akin approximately to Lawrence's in *The Rainbow*, to ride language to some transcendent, some extra-linguistic truth. The novel is not primarily about Omensetter; the man is only the nemesis of Furber (as well as of Tott and Pimber) and the catalyst for his actions and words. Furber's precious constructions, his "beautiful barriers of words," and his rantings, his not so beautiful barriers, are placed beside Brackett's stolid, implacable taciturnity. The word "stone" is frequently used in connection with Omensetter, whose muteness speaks more eloquently for Jethro's futility than the clergyman's words do, or Omensetter's words could. Not accidentally, the word that appears most often in conjunction with Furber is "futility."

Like Percival in Woolf's *The Waves*, Omensetter has no monologue to himself. His presence, though, permeates the novel speaking silently and monopolizing Tott, Pimber, and Furber. For Tott, inveterate story-teller and liar, the memory of Omensetter provides him the chance to tell the long story, which never gets told. For Pimber, Omensetter is a kind of Lena Grove figure, inarticulate but intuitively grasping what is right, without recourse to logic or language. The language associated with him is saturated with images of nature and animals. The sentences he utters, and they are few, are comprised mainly of monosyllabic words. They stand as an indictment of Furber's incessant verbalizing. By contrast, like Robert Browning's prolix monologuists, Furber is a compulsive talker, inwardly via stream-of-consciousness prose and outwardly in a tenuously rational manner. His section fluctuates between an indulgent, impressionistic, ribald language (the inner), and a circumspect language (the outer). The former, which manifests the sexual and religious turbulence within him, threatens to drown the latter. Furber's language games subsume him. Imagining contact with "Fatty Ruth" or a sexual encounter with any other woman, Furber asserts that rendering such moments in language surpasses the reality of them: "words were superior; they maintained a superior control; they touched without your touching; they were at once the bait, the hook, the line, the pole, and the water in between" (OL, p.113). The Mrs. Kinsman who evokes so many memories and whose proper name initiates a great many rhymes and word games is one who is ravished verbally by Furber. He vicariously relates sensual pagan rites to her, the telling of which is for him the moment of fruition: "These words of his—for her they were only the prelude to Lohengrin, but for him they were the thing, the actual opera itself" (OL, p.163). Furber's amatory skills manifest themselves in the wielding of discreet verbs, light nouns, delicate conjunctions.

Furber's romance with language ultimately drives him mad because it cannot mesh or allow him to mesh with the world. The reason he hates Omensetter so is the ease with which that man is at one with nature. "Whatever Omensetter does," he muses, "he does without desire in the ordinary sense, with a kind of abandon, a stony mindlessness that makes me always think of Eden" (OL, p.126). Mixed with his hatred of Omensetter is Furber's desire to be like the man. He impersonates the primitive, masculine Omensetter in his encounter with Lucy Pimber. When she chuckles after he says, "I am Brackett Omensetter" (OL, p.128), in an unnaturally resonant voice, Jethro beats her.

Omensetter's taciturnity, though, is something that ill fits Furber.

Furber's imagined conversations with Pike are skilful and witty, but interminable; yet they are his sustenance. After Pike provides him with the paradox, "the way the world is, you have to look down to see up" (*OL*, p. 99), Furber concocts a host of clever paradoxes in this vein:

> And versions of it began to flutter wildly through his head. You have to look round to see straight. Good enough. Useful. And the rough places plain. But all that's geometry. But it measures the earth. You have to go slow to catch up. Eat to get thin? no, but fast to grow fat, that was a fine one. Then lose to win? Fail to succeed? Risky. Stop to begin. The form made noiseless music — lumly lum lum or lum-lee-lee lum — like fill to empty, every physical extreme. (*OL*, p. 99)

Word games proliferate. Every face and name of Gilean's townfolk provides him with the stuff of an irreverent, rhythmical digression. Frequently, Furber has to wrestle with the logic of his sermons and diurnal conversations, so engrossed is he in his inner verbal gymnastics. Persons' names trigger alliteration and rhymes: sour Susan, Pat the Fat, curdled Carol, Philly Kinsman the famous bandsman; they also prompt verses: "Samantha Totty...grew her nose...in her potty...like a rose" (*OL*, p. 78). Words also release a concatenation of associative responses: "Inward — in a word — inwardly — in his innards" (*OL*, p. 175) and "The number of the noise...so numerous...numberless....numb" (*OL*, p. 171). Words are relished for their sound, their physical properties (Lo-Lee-Ta): Cath-all-oh-cizz-um, See-cree-shun, Nay-ked-ness. Once a motif or word game is picked up, it is retained throughout the novel. Often it is repeated throughout the monologue just as the tapping of the blind man's cane appears occasionally in James Joyce's *Ulysses*. There is, for example, the animal motif which is initiated by "Camel. Hump where the head is. That's why. Two humps: two heads. The heads of infants — several. Or embracing lovers" (*OL*, p. 141). The third section of his monologue is replete with the names of animals which Furber incessantly lists. Also, Furber names cities beginning with the letter "C," then constantly refers to them as a way of returning to the logical development of his outer speech.

Despite his fancy, Furber is never far from madness. His virtuoso performance with words, constructing his syntax from the logic of his imagination, never leads him out of the prison-house of language. His tenuous constructs always threaten to collapse — "Like a water-strider, Furber rode a thin film of sense" (*OL*, p. 174). To find through language an integrated, harmonious existence with the world is denied him. "To find and utter the proper words, the *logoi spermatakoi*... that was Plato's game" (*OL*, p. 168), not his own. What Pynchon calls "the direct, epileptic Word" is missing. Furber, blighted by the contemporary perception of language, is trapped in its labyrinth, a play-field, which has neither centre nor exit. Without an absolute to which to refer, not even the religion he preaches, Furber is doomed. "He tried to rally his thoughts and form them in unassailable squares, but not a line would hold, they broke ahead of any shooting, and the Logos wandered disloyally off, alone, rudely hiccoughing and chewing on pieces of raw potato, looking surly and dangerous. No book but Nature is the word of God" (*OL*, p. 85). And it was Omensetter's luck intuitively to approach nearer to it than Furber could ever get.

Jethro Furber is a guilt-ridden Humbert Humbert. Although he enjoys his dazzling language games as much as Humbert does, he is unable to content himself with "the refuge of art" (Nabokov, p. 281), which is the only immortality Humbert and Lolita are permitted to share. Each of Gass's narrators is caught in the play of language and the world, seeking to contain world within words; however neat the constructions, the subsumption of world by words is never fully possible. Signifieds resist signifiers, however beautiful those barriers of words are, however marvellously they mesh. The narrator of "Order of Insects," for example, is a housewife who discerns, in dead roaches discovered on her carpet, "gracious order, wholeness and divinity....O my husband, they are a terrible disease."[22] Order, wholeness, and divinity, because they are of her making, constitute a threat to her quotidian life. She must choose between being a housewife or an artist, an unconscious participant in the game of the world or a creator of her own:

> Strange. Absurd. I am the wife of the house. This point of view I tremble in is the point of view of a god, and I feel certain, somehow, that could I give myself entirely to it, were I not continuing a woman, I could disarm my life, find peace and order everywhere; and I lie by my husband and I touch his arm and consider the temptation. But I am a woman. I am not worthy.... Peace. How can I think of such ludicrous things — beauty and peace, the dark soul of the world — for I am the wife of the house, concerned for the rug, tidy and punctual, surrounded by blocks. (*HHC*, p. 171)

45

The wife flees the fiction of her making, reverting to the constructs that pre-exist her, her socially ordained role.

Like the housewife, the narrator of "Mrs. Mean," another story from *In the Heart of the Heart of the Country*, begins totally committed to his construct; however, he, too, ultimately abandons his fabrication. The narrator calls her Mrs. Mean because "it suggests the glassy essence, the grotesquerie of Type" (*HHC*, p. 80); it brings her into the world of art, into a design of his own making. There she can embody meanness "with the formality and grandeur of Being" (*HHC*, p. 80). The struggle for the narrator is to subordinate Mrs. Mean's activities, to place them in his story. Whereas the woman is active ("Her pace is furious" [*HHC*, p. 88]), he attempts to achieve stasis ("I feel I have succeeded to the idleness of God" [*HHC*, p. 88]). In the elaborate world of his words, Mrs. Mean and her children probably battle more seriously than parents and children do; also, he makes the woman into the ogre she may or may not be. When a certain Mr. Wallace attempts to break into the order he has brought to the house and the people he is re-creating ("a juncture, I must confess, that had not occurred to me although I sometimes fancy I am master of the outside chance" [*HHC*, p. 108]), the narrator undertakes to excoriate that gentleman with a Borgesian disquisition on moles:

> I discoursed upon them: causes, underflesh connections, cosmic parallels, relations to divinity....I referred to the moles of beauty, to those of avarice, cunning, gluttony and lust, to those which, when touched, made the eyes water, the ears itch, or caused the prick to stand and the shyest maid to flower. My fancy soared. I related moles and maps, moles and mountains, moles and the elements of interior earth. Oh it was wondrous done. (*HHC*, p. 110)

More tenacious than the housewife of "Order of Insects," the narrator is nonetheless of the same ilk: obsessed by his constructs, lured by them. He is also restive with his language play, wishing to make his words flesh. At the end of the story he yearns to be a part of the story he has shaped of Means, Cramms, Ames, "to be the clothes that lie against their skins, to shift with them, absorb their smells" (*HHC*, p. 118).

Another story in the same collection traces a similar situation. The most lyrical of all Gass's fictions, "Icicles" has as its narrator an idiosyncratic real estate salesman for whom icicles are talismanic. As farfetched as Fender's obsession appears to be, it is paradigmatic of the shaping powers of word, the malleability of world. ("Prop-purr-tee. A lovely sound. He hauled the door open" [*HHC*, p. 151].) Fender's logophilia, which always spawns richness and rhythms, produces something, however, which is as vulnerable as the icicles on his houses are to neighbourhood children. Its cleverness does not provide solidity. Forebodingly, at the end of the story, "it was as though, suddenly, a fist had opened, and they [the children] came down the hill like a snowfall of rocks" (*HHC*, p. 162). His constructions are being threatened. Finally, Gass's novella, *Willie Master's Lonesome Wife*, which contains a compendium of techniques for denying the mimetic properties of fiction, insists more trenchantly and ecstatically than any of his other fictions on the life language leads within itself. Men may penetrate Willie's wife, the sensuous narrator, with all the ardour they might lavish on a life-size, inflatable doll; nonetheless, she retains her faith in a renewed poetry of form and language which transforms her lament into a positive assertion, the energetic, rhapsodic "yes" of Joyce's Molly Bloom. Uncompromisingly she also utters Gass's dictum about character in fiction: "These words are all I am. Believe me.... Not even the Dane is any more than that."[23]

In each of the fictions discussed above, then, Gass explores the discrepancy between world and word. His narrators erect tenuous but enticing structures with words, which clash with the worlds they inhabit, a paradigm that recurs in the fiction of Hawkes, Nabokov, and Coover as well. The principle embedded in the machinations of narrators and novelists is the construction of worlds that are, maintains Gass, tantalizingly approximate to but not imitative of the world in which we live. That is all language allows one to do. Yet man is an inveterate and persistent structure maker, this, indeed, being one of his most seminal activities. He creates systems, institutions, cosmologies, philosophies, theologies, none of which encapsulates the world, all of which attempt to order it and inject value into it. Gass's kind of fiction is overwhelmingly anti-mimetic, denying that language, specifically the language of literature, captures experience or delineates some external reality; on the contrary, as Gass emphatically states, "there are no descriptions in fiction, there are only constructions" (*FFL*, p. 17). Those constructions are essential for understanding a world they ineluctably alter. As Gass has asserted in a recent essay, "Representation and the War for Reality," "to look on Being bare, we must strip it of signs."[24] Such a task mutes commentary which must inevitably falsify. Language, for Gass and other metafictionists, is not the instrument with which one cuts away the dross to bare "Being"; rather, it alters that inarticulable essence.

The narrators in Gass's fiction attempt relentlessly to yoke signs and "Being," to replace an inchoate world with their noetic, their verbal structures. The same impulse prods Barthelme's Snow White to utter her lament, "O I wish there were some words in the world that were not the words I always hear."[25] Perceiving a mundane, banal milieu around her, she betrays a yearning for the kind of language play that has not turned "Being" into a cliché, into the jejune phrasing that has constrained the world. In this sense, creative use of language produces liberation from reified perceptions of the world and concomitantly from sterile visions of America. The attempt on the part of the metafictionists and their protagonists is to undermine the status of those false documents that have become ensconced as reality. The purpose is not to supplant those documents with truer ones (though occasional thrasonical narrators try); rather, it is to expose the palpable fictiveness of those and any documents that purport to explain world, that masquerade as truth rather than as construct.

Such an engagement with false documents is vital not only in epistemological terms, but also in social terms. Monolithic America and its ideology, and concomitantly its reality, are reduced to the status of Vonnegut's bad fiction. Thus, although Gass's characters such as Furber, Willie Master's lonesome wife, and the melancholy and bitter narrator of "In the Heart of the Heart of the Country" do not confront overtly and didactically the American identity, their dilemmas pertain to the status of any identity that has been accorded ontological security. Coover's J. Henry Waugh, it should be noted, though he, too, betrays no evident biases towards or even interest in political dimensions of reality, does engage the same duality: the bland world already shaped for him and the enriched fictive world he creates. The former milieu is one that is saturated by, to quote Doctorow, the "language of the regime." That language, among other properties it has, dispenses facts, imbuing such terms as soul or democracy or identity crisis, for example, with validity; Doctorow's language of freedom calls into question these facts. The power of this language lies in its ability to be marshalled into false documents as real as but other than those documents upon which the power of the regime confers truth. Doctorow writes,

> The novelist's opportunity to do his work today is increased
> by the power of the regime to which he finds himself in

opposition. As clowns in the circus imitate the aerialists and tight-rope walkers, first for laughs and then so that it can be seen that they do it better, we have it in us to compose false documents more valid, more real, more truthful than the "true" documents of the politicians or the journalists or the psychologists. Novelists know explicitly that the world in which we live is still to be formed and that reality is amenable to any construction that is placed upon it. It is a world made for liars and we are born liars.[26]

Gass's most well-known short story, the often anthologized "In the Heart of the Heart of the Country," sharply and vividly expresses the clash of the two warring camps with their attendant ideologies and languages. The directory of middle America is clustered in separate sections of the story labelled "Data," "More Vital Data," and "Final Vital Data": the clubs ("The IOOF, FFF, VFW, WCTU, WSCS, 4-H, 40 and 8, Psi Iota Chi, and PTA" [HHC, p. 198]), the businesses ("There are two restaurants here and a tearoom. two bars. one bank..." [HHC, p. 177]), and so on. There is the midwestern character succinctly and sardonically defined: "Sports, politics, and religion are the three passions of the badly educated. They are the Midwest's open sores" (HHC, p. 197). This harsh and skeletal portrait is drawn of "B...a small town fastened to a field in Indiana" (HHC, p. 172). Ironically recalling William Butler Yeats's Byzantium, the refuge of the artist who experiences an ecstasy free of "the fury and the mire of human veins,"[27] the locale at the heart of the heart of this narrator's country is a heartless place, the Midland City of Breakfast of Champions.

The poet-narrator battles, though, to rejuvenate self and country in language. Of his milieu he writes, "there's law: to rule...to regulate...to rectify. I cannot write the poetry of such proposals, the poetry of politics..." (HHC, p. 175). Despite being lovelorn and despondent, he musters language ("Similes dangle like baubles from me" [HHC, p. 191]) into his own Byzantium. "I keep wondering," he says of one of B's inhabitants, "whether, given time, I might not someday find a figure in our language which would serve him faithfully, and furnish his poverty and loneliness richly out" (HHC, p. 190). Superbly, Gass provides in the narrator's monologue the contrast between middle American clichés ("the children will be taught to read and warned against Communism" [HHC, p. 187]) and his own literary constructs ("A bush in the excitement of its roses could not have bloomed so beautifully as you did then. It was a look I'd like

49

to give this page. For that is poetry: to bring within about, to change" [*HHC*, p.197]).

Yet, as in most of Gass's fiction, there is not only the disinterested clash of the languages of the regime and of freedom. There is also a poignancy about, a mythopoeic nostalgia for, the healing of the dislocation of bare "Being" and signs. Too much of a postmodernist and too much of a semioticist to accept the juxtaposition of word and world, Gass, nonetheless, betrays a yearning for such an endeavour. His narrator in "In the Heart of the Heart of the Country" is predisposed to the logocentrism that is vital to humanism; however, he knows what Mas'ud Zavarzadeh calls the informing principle of semiotics, "in which concepts and ideas do not exist prior to and independent of their place in a system of signification."[28] Poetry over and over again is berated by the narrator — "Childhood is a lie of poetry" (*HHC*, p.205) and "It is another lie of poetry" (*HHC*, p.202) — because regardless of the ravishing or seemingly efficacious power of words, they remain separated from action. Pithily he says, "Body equals being, and if your weight goes down, you are the less" (*HHC*, p.202). In other words, the compensation of language is limited for this person, bereft of his loved one. His *cri de coeur* is a Yeatsian one for immersion in "the foul rag-and-bone shop of the heart."[29] He wishes to acquire the poetry of his cat for whom there is not the split between "Being" and signs: "Claws, not metrical schema, poetry his paws; while smoothing...smoothing...smoothing roughly, his tongue laps its neatness. O Mr. Tick, I know you; you are an electrical penis" (*HHC*, pp.184–85). He also celebrates the mute, active loving he and his former mate shared: "Our union was a singing, though we were silent in the songs we sang like single notes are silent in a symphony" (*HHC*, p.185).

"In the Heart of the Heart of the Country" not only dissects the innards of self and state, but it also examines the role language and form play vis-à-vis both. Instead of a linear unwinding of the poet's interaction with his place, Gass presents the story in an atomized fashion, short, terse sequences labelled variously "A Place," "Politics," "People," "My House, This Place and Body," and so on. The effect is to retard sequential narrative, to place prominently in the foreground the distance between event and transcription of event, between bare "Being" and sign. That Gass, more than other metafictionists, divulges a Romantic, Whitmanesque yearning for the congruence of world and word in no way undermines his trenchant grasp of the impossibility of such a yoking. His fiction and theory, nowhere more sensuously and aptly than in "In the Heart of the Heart of the Country," reveal the following: a disgust with reified American values, the cathectic America of Chapter One; a distrust of the language that transmits such a vision; a disbelief in the status of character or selfhood; a disenchantment with the appurtenances of conventional fiction-making. Each of these seemingly disparate dimensions of his art and criticism coheres in a rejection of the positivistic, in a pervasive notion of reality and language's place in that scheme.

Gass shares with Coover, Barthelme, Pynchon, and other contemporary American writers of fiction, as well as with Derrida and the others associated with him who are mentioned in Chapter One, a radical refusal of what Foucault would call a whole episteme. Two antithetical modes of writing fiction and criticism and, indeed, of living in the world clash here. Insofar as literary theory and criticism are concerned, J. Hillis Miller separated the two camps into canny and uncanny critics. Canny critics are "lulled by the promise of a rational ordering of literary study on the basis of solid advances in scientific knowledge about language" (Zavarzadeh, p. 329). They are positivistic, certain of the legitimacy and veracity of textual interpretation and sure of the solid statuses of text and world. (E. D. Hirsch, with the writing of *Validity in Interpretation* and *Aims in Interpretation*, would be an extreme example of such a critic.) Uncanny critics, on the other hand, have a far less assured notion about textual interpretation and the firm boundaries of text and world. In reading them, "the bottom drops out, or there is an 'abyssing,' an insight one can almost grasp or recognize as part of the familiar landscape of the mind, but not quite, as though the mental eye could not quite bring the material into lucid focus" (Zavarzadeh, p. 329). Undermined by uncanny critics are transcribable meanings. Obviously, Gass's affinities are with the uncanny critics. Indeed, one could call the metafictionists uncanny novelists in the sense of the word Miller proposes.

In two virulent and acerbic essays, "Even if, by All the Oxen in the World" and "The Artist and Society," which conclude *Fiction and the Figures of Life*, Gass uncannily, in both senses of that word, decentres mass man's solidity and selfhood. "Even if, by All the Oxen in the World" is an attack on popular culture and the mind that culture shapes.

The working consciousness...is narrow, shuttered by utility, its transitions eased by habit past reflection like a thief. Impulses from without or from within must use some strength to reach us, we do not go out to them. Machines are made this way. Alert as lights and aimed like guns, they only see the circle of their barrels. (*FFL*, p. 269)

Gass's sense of the utilitarian consciousness is that it is mass-produced, a clichéd, programmed vehicle. Devoid of substance, it is moulded from without, producing a person whose "hopes are purchased, his voice prerecorded, his play...mechanical, the roles typed, their lines trite..." (*FFL*, p. 271). Repeatedly, Gass insists that what passes for consciousness is largely induced externally rather than formed internally; concomitantly the language produced by such a consciousness is prefabricated and predictable: "he spends at least a week each year in touring and a month in memorizing lies — lies moral, religious, and political — he beats the drum or shouts hurray on cue, he wears a neon nightie, swallows pills, and chews his woman's nipples now because a book he's read has told him that he ought to..." (*FFL*, p. 271).

Such a pastiche, such a composite is not only Gass's summation of character, it is also a metaphor of an America that has eschewed any sense of innovative fictions for facile and stylized ones. The whole of the metafictionist's enterprise impinges here, yoking prefabricated character with prefabricated country. Add prefabricated fictions and one sees how notions of self, country, and literature combine seamlessly; how the conventions of each are regarded as having become ensconced as norms, as absolutes. In "Even if, by All the Oxen in the World" Gass assaults, ever so caustically, what for him are the arbitrary and overly rigidifed conventions and modes of living that have become value-laden. The vitriol is continued in "The Artist and Society":

Have you met a typical non-person lately? Then say hello, now, to your neighbor. He may be male, but his facial expressions have been put on like lipstick and eyelashes. His greeting is inevitable; so is his interest in the weather. He always smiles; he speaks only in clichés; and his opinions...are drearily predictable. He has nothing but good to say of people; he collects his wisdom like dung from a Digest; he likes to share his experiences with "folks," and recite the plots of movies. (*FFL*, p. 283)

Although Gass's hortatory and strident remarks are directed primarily against the narcotizing dimensions of popular culture, his antidote throughout these two essays is art — not mimetic art, though.

Rather, his art is an art of liars, of convention breakers. Like Doctorow he champions those subversive formal dimensions of art that undermine accepted standards and values. Works of art, Gass writes, are not important "for the messages they may contain, not because they expose slavery or cry hurrah for the worker, although such messages in their place and time might be important, but because they insist more than most on their own reality" (*FFL*, p. 282). The contrast is between a world in which modes of living and mores, palpably false though they may be, are acceded to and a world of fiction, which confronts "us the way few people dare to: completely, openly, at once" (*FFL*, p. 283). The climactic irony, of course, is that the latter world is more vital than the former one: "We take our breaths. We fornicate and feed. But Hamlet has his history in the heart, and none of us will ever be as real, as vital, as complex and living as he is — a total creature of the stage" (*FFL*, p. 283).

In other fine essays such as "Philosophy and the Form of Fiction," "The Medium of Fiction," and "The Concept of Character in Fiction" Gass's enemies are more purely literary — namely, the shibboleths of prose fiction. Of the primacy of language as opposed to events in fiction, he writes that it is "shocking, really. It's as though you had discovered that your wife were made of rubber: the bliss of all those years, the fears...from sponge" (*FFL*, p. 27). Of the obsession with realistic characters and their realistic dilemmas, Gass is contemptuous. The link between conventional self and conventional prose fiction and their deleterious consequences is sharply etched in Gass's theoretical essays. It, also, prepares one for a telling dismissal of America's status which is devalued and undermined; in contrast to Canadian writers' militant adherence to the Canadian identity, nationalism is reviled, scorned as a false community of enthusiasts. Those who espouse their country's ethos, who accept its legitimacy as anything except something created for political convenience are akin to those who have been shaped by popular culture:

> People who have seen the same game, heard the same comedians, danced to the same din, read the same detectives, can form a community of enthusiasts whose exchange of feelings not only produces the most important secondary effect of popular culture (the culture hero and his worship services), but also helps persuade people that their experiences were real, reinforces judgments of their values, and confirms their addiction. (*FFL*, p. 272)

Whereas Canadian writers have banded together in the Canadian Writers' Union and have formulated tenets (one of which excludes miscegenation of a literary kind) which imply a keen sense of country, American writers reject that role. Gass is in the forefront of the metafictionists who are far less shrill than Kesey or Ginsberg. Whereas Canadian writers see themselves contributing to their society, American writers regard their roles as far more combative and antagonistic. Gass writes, "the artist is...an enemy of every ordinary revolution..." (*FFL*, p. 287). Clearly, Gass, the uncanny critic of both literature and culture, undermines everything. Statehood, selfhood, and the canons of prose fiction are tyrannies. In his fiction, world and word clash; in his criticism, cliché and creativeness are at odds.

Because of his relentless wit and dextrous prose, Gass is metafiction's most lucid and incisive spokesperson. (His supremacy remains unrivalled despite his limited output and his recent tortuous efforts in "The Tunnel" to maintain and extend his labyrinthine style.) Given the occasionally perspicacious critical forays of Barth in sundry literate interviews as well as in "The Literature of Exhaustion"[30] and "The Literature of Replenishment"[31] and among other articles, a piece such as Doctorow's "False Documents," Gass's achievement is noteworthy. He is seminal to this study, firstly, because he relentlessly attacks those conservative dimensions of life and art — nationalistic and personal identities, as well as mimetic art — that are staples of Canada's social and literary context. Secondly, he articulates those postmodernist precepts that have been so readily assimilated by a phalanx of American writers. The receptivity to Gass's pronouncements and also the fervent backlash they have produced attest to the repugnance of most of the American literati to be subsumed in some cultural mission.

If William Gass can be regarded as the most insightful and vitriolic of metafiction's theoreticians, Robert Coover can be seen to be its most persistently nasty practitioner. Pummelled while making a movie of an anti-Vietnam war demonstration in Iowa City, Iowa, and subsequently deprived of his film in dubious circumstances, Coover forsook the United States for Mexico and England and returned to the United States only after a lengthy hiatus largely at his son's behest. Works such as *A Political Fable*, *A Theological Position*, and, most prominently, *The Public Burning* skewer the arbitrary trappings of state, self, and literature, which Gass reviles. In one of his few non-fictional pieces, "The Last Quixote: Marginal Notes on the Gospel According to Samuel Beckett," Coover extols Beckett for his longheld adversity to the objects of Gass's rage. Wittily, he cites Beckett as an exemplar "when Christ and Tennessee Williams failed....Of course, he also pandered to my own awkward fumblings with the inconsonance between words and their referents."[32]

More generally he lauds Beckett for having shown him, he writes, a way "of making art, without affirmation" (Coover, p. 136). Art, for Coover, deflates rather than inflates, gives the lie to the constructs produced not only in literary but also in social senses. Coover understands Beckett's art as an uncompromising and unrelenting disengagement from system building. It is here that Beckett becomes the cynosure of postmodernists whose major characteristic is scepticism towards the ontological status of man's products, including himself. This should not be construed as nihilism. There is appreciation, richly Borgesian, of man, the inventor of cosmos, values, ethics, norms; however, there is also a refusal to accept his products in any, except semiotic, terms. Certainly, they are rejected as absolutes. Of Beckett, Coover writes, "He wants no more vain efforts to extend art's repertory, this 'straining to enlarge the statement of compromise,' choosing instead 'to submit wholly to' (imitate?) 'the incoercible absence of relation...between the artist and his occasion'" (Coover, p. 137). In more specific literary terms Beckett is also acknowledged as an innovator insofar as prose fiction is concerned. Coover asserts that he "undoes all our ancient notions about character, plot (history), setting ("'— but to hell with all this fucking scenery,'" grumps Malone) and his entire opus might be thought of, from one point of view, as the relentless annihilation of 'point of view'" (Coover, p. 138).

Coover's entire opus confronts a common enemy. In his fiction the staples of prose fiction are refused or revamped. His work is also that of a quintessentially postmodernist writer, one whose sensibility includes a distinctively anarchistic dimension that belongs to the postmodernist perspective. Reified, rule governed states and states of mind receive a sustained assault at Coover's hands. Although *The Public Burning* is Coover's most explicitly political and most vituperative engagement with rigidified structures, all his work is combative in aesthetic, philosophical, lexical, and social terms. More viciously than Nabokov who chortles about muddle-crass American manners, more searingly than Vonnegut who renders in an adolescent manner the bad fiction America has become, Coover vitiates cultural and artistic clichés and stagnation. In the dedicatory preface to Cervantes in

Pricksongs and Descants, he celebrates the following qualities of Cervantes' stories: "they struggled against the unconscious mythic residue in human life and sought to synthesize the unsynthesizable, sallied forth against adolescent thought-modes and exhausted artforms, and returned home with new complexities."[33] True to the radical nature of his master's stories, Coover's stories uncompromisingly attack suffocating ideologies and attenuated art forms.

The residue of our culture's stories — theological, mythical, fabulous — suffers most grievously at Coover's metafictive hands; notions of mimesis, causality, and objectivity are also ruthlessly disrupted. Point of view, too, receives Beckett-like undermining: in "A Pedestrian Accident," Paul steps off a curb and is run over by a transport truck. "He lay perpendicular to the length of the truck, under the trailer, just to the rear of the truck's second of three sets of wheels. All of him was under the truck but his head and shoulders" (*Pricksongs*, pp. 183–84). The ensuing commotion and rescue operations, which occupy the rest of the story, are all narrated from Paul's supine, limited perspective. "The Sentient Lens" is a trilogy, each vignette of which presents the clash between objective lens and unresolvable action, an opposition that is delineated in Julio Cortazar's fine story, "Blow-Up." What is championed rather than denigrated in Coover's story is the freedom to construct new worlds. "The Hat Act" provides the most crystalline image of this: the story of a magician not bound by conventional tricks, it is quite simply a metaphor for the artist who can create fantastical, new realms, violating, if and when it pleases him, the supposedly normative operations of reality and literature. Stereotypic characters such as the lovely, young assistant, the abashed country boy, and two hulking he-men perform stereotypic deeds, which are, respectively, sexy, clumsy, and macho. These events are interspersed with equally rote audience responses such as laughter, horror, and approbation to reveal how manipulable audiences are and also how easily authors can produce materials made from formulae. "The Hat Act" gives an insight into the relationship of artist and audience, which Gass defines in "Philosophy and the Form of Fiction":

> In the story of Mary, if Mary dies, the novelist killed her, her broken heart did not. The author of any popular serial knows, as Dickens did, that to the degree he makes his world real to his readers, to that degree they will acknowledge his authorship; hold him responsible; and beg him to make the world good, although evil seems present in it; beg him to bring

all to a moral and materially glorious close, in clouds and hallelujahs. (*FFL*, pp. 18-19)

For Coover, as for Gass, the staples of fiction can be somnambulistic or pernicious. The alternately wily and clichéd magician of "The Hat Act" reveals the deliberate quality of the artist's enterprise, debunking the seemingly seamless vision of realism.

In "The Magic Poker" Coover deals with the same motif, this time presenting a conscious, manipulative authorial presence, which alerts the reader to the artifice inherent in realistic fiction. The process of creation is highlighted in this story. Karen, her thrice divorced sister, the atavistic caretaker's son, and his suave civilized antithesis — together on an otherwise deserted island, they are the stuff of a heavily suspenseful tale. However, Coover's magic poker, his pen, is the potent master of the wrought-iron poker, around which the island's mysteries centre. Coover writes tales of monsters and fairy princes, together with realistic stories, in order to undercut the development of each and all of these narrative threads. Predominant in the story is the "I" of the narrator who shapes and plays with his material—"I wander the island, inventing it....I deposit shadows and dampness....I impose a hot midday silence" (*Pricksongs*, p. 20). Coover intrudes in other ways to force his reader's awareness. Should the reader, for example, become engrossed in the excremental vision embodied in the caretaker's son, the narrator interpolates:

> Wait a minute, this is getting out of hand! What happened to that poker, I was doing much better with the poker, I had something going there, archetypal and even maybe beautiful, a blend of eros and wisdom, sex and sensibility, music and myth. But what am I going to do with shit in a rusty teakettle? No, no, there's nothing to be gained by burdening our fabrications with impieties. Enough that the skin of the world is littered with our contentious artifice....(*Pricksongs*, p. 30)

Contentious artifice is an ideological straitjacket masked as natural order. It is the shibboleth Coover attacks in all his fiction, the historically rooted *The Public Burning* and the less libellous but equally uncompromising *Pricksongs and Descants, A Theological Position* and *The Universal Baseball Association, Inc.: J. Henry Waugh, Prop.* Again in "The Magic Poker" Coover confronts another facet of that shibboleth as it is manifested in art: realism and all the paraphernalia of the well-wrought tale:

I am disappearing. You have no doubt noticed. Yes, and by some no doubt calculable formula of event and pagination. But before we drift apart to a distance beyond the reach of confessions (though I warn you: like Zeno's turtle, I am with you always), listen: it's just as I feared, my invented island is really taking its place in world geography. Why this island sounds very much like the old Dahlberg place on Jackfish Island up on Rainy Lake, people say, and I wonder: can it be happening? Someone tells me: I understand somebody bought the place recently and plans to fix it up, maybe put a resort there or something. On *my* island? Extraordinary! — and yet it seems possible. I look on a map: yes, there's Rainy Lake, there's Jackfish Island. Who invented this map? Well, I must have surely. And the Dahlbergs, too, of course, and the people who told me about them. Yes, and perhaps tomorrow I will invent Chicago and Jesus Christ and the history of the moon. Just as I have invented you, dear reader.... (*Pricksongs*, p. 40)

The tone here is Nabokovian, deliberately taunting the reader for whom literature is something other than a lexical playfield.

In "The Elevator" and "The Babysitter," Coover presents the reader with all the story lines available to him rather than developing one of them. They are juxtaposed so that the one true story and with it causality and linearity are fractured and obscured. Descents into Hell, existential confrontations with death, permutations of sexual themes — these are superimposed upon each other to undercut all but the authorial play with these counters. In other short fictions by Coover, worn out or narrow perceptions of the world are criticized as rigorously as are antiquated perceptions of art. "Morris in Chains," for instance, inveighs against the sociologist's version of reality. The stifling technological culture, which enslaves one with data and objectivity, is regarded as insidious. Morris, the idiosyncratic Pan-figure of the story, is hunted: "[his] least event was recorded on notepad, punchcard, film, tape. Observers reported his noises, odors, motions, choices, acquisitions, excretions, emissions, irritations, dreams" (*Pricksongs*, p. 55). For Morris, "it's the motherin insane are free!" (*Pricksongs*, p. 60). Though the format is different, "Love Scene" presents enslavement to another of the old perceptions. Despite the Voice's attempt to invest the love act with new meaning, new vitality, its course recapitulates "man, the whole western world, all that lunacy, all that history, A to Z...."[34] Just as Morris is enchained, the Voice does not succeed in its desire to recreate the love act freshly.

Coover deals most mercilessly with theological stories. "The Brother" retells the story of Noah's ark from the point of view of Noah's brother who is wilfully left to perish in the flood in order to fulfil the great design. "A Theological Position" parodies the virgin birth and scrutinizes Christian precepts through a mouthpiece that just happens to be the "virgin's" vagina:

> CUNT: You love to fog up the ether with your own hokum nimbi, debase the living world with phony mystifications sprung spookily from your geometries and glossolalias, but how you shy from something so simple as communication with your own gametes! Hey, I'm calling to your balls, boys!35

The *Universal Baseball Association* also contains diverse theological speculations, rendered in language as inimitably visceral as that contained in the above example. "'I must agree with our distinguished folklorist and foremost witness to the ontological revelations of the patterns of history,' intercedes... Professor Costen Migod McCamish, Doctor of Nostology and Research Specialist in the Etiology of Homo Ludens, 'and have come to the conclusion that God exists and he is a nut.'"36

The *Universal Baseball Association* is the story of J. Henry Waugh, JHWH, the novel's god-figure. So dissatisfied is Waugh with the flaccid and mundane world that he lives and works in as an accountant with the firm of Dunkelmann, Zauber, and Zifferblatt that he eschews the Zifferblatt universe for his own construct, a baseball world that he peoples, plays, and protects. As an artist Waugh proffers his own world in which he can shape history, a vital word which recurs throughout this novel as it does throughout *The Public Burning*. Of the reality he finds distasteful, Waugh muses: "The bus was jammed, they had to stand. People jostled, rammed them moistly toward the rear. Rain drummed on the roof. If skyscrapers were penis-prisons, what were the buses? The efferent tubes? The driver barked orders. Passengers protested at the shoving" (*UBA*, p. 49). It is a world that contains only quotidian value and significance. Coover articulates this by having Waugh demand of his cohort, "At 4:34 on a wet November afternoon, Lou Engel boarded a city bus and spilled water from his hat brim on a man's newspaper. Is that history?" (*UBA*, p. 50). After Lou answers feebly, Henry queries, "Who's writing it down?" (*UBA*, p. 50). The tenacity with which J. Henry shapes and maintains his other world is prefigured in this bit of by-play. His Universal Baseball Association provides him with the artist's chance to create a patterned, ordered, beautiful world of the imagination. Baseball — J. Henry says of baseball stadiums that they and not European churches are the real American holy places — provides Coover with the metaphor for this world. As Roger Angell reveals exultantly in *The Summer Game*, baseball is a game of pattern, of symmetry, of stateliness, which has the added lure of being quantifiable, measurable in the reams of statistics that give to baseball its voluminous history. Moreover, it is a world to which J. Henry, man the structure-maker, gives meaning by writing its history, the Book rather than a book. "Into the Book went the whole UBA, everything from statistics to journalistic dispatches, from seasonal analyses to general baseball theory. Everything, in short, worth keeping" (*UBA*, p.55). To emphasize the encyclopaedic and Biblical character of the UBA's official archives, Coover writes that J. Henry chose record books that had good rag content for durability and pens that contained permanent black ink.

Despite Henry's record keeping zeal and his god-like beneficence and care of the players whom he creates and whom he follows on and off the playing field until their deaths — he even vomits "a red-and-golden rainbow arc of half-curded pizza over his Association" (*UBA*, p.202) as a covenant — his world stagnates and degenerates. Coover's restive and disruptive sensibility manifests itself in the last chapter. By concluding the book with the eighth instead of the ninth chapter Coover refuses to provide a harmonious organization and pattern to his baseball book. In that final chapter the game has been going on for many years and the system's entropy has greatly increased. Waugh / Yahweh, the God-figure, is absent and only badly understood; attenuated tradition, ritual, mythology, and history sustain order in the UBA's civilization. Despite the spate of interpretations and sects, which have sprung up around the seminal events in the history of the UBA, the beaning of Damon Rutherford and the concomitant deliberate felling of Jock Casey, those incidents, so redolent of Christian and Western lore, are re-enacted. One of the participants meditates in the following way on the long since obscured actual occurrence: "Or maybe it just happened. Weirdly, independently, meaninglessly. Another accident in a chain of accidents: worse even than invention. Invention...implies a need and need implies purpose; accident implies nothing, nothing at all, and nothing is the one thing that scares Hardy Ingram" (*UBA*, pp.224–25). By means of a welter of punning, which is profuse in Chapter Eight, Coover reiterates his major points: that a labyrinthine, Derridean verbal universe and clashing philosophies which cancel out each other allow for no resolution, no absolutes; that man must constantly rejuvenate myth and language; that reconsideration and reconceptualization of reality are essential to the vitality of man the structure-maker.

Urged to conserve tradition by one of the participants in the ritual, "well, legend, I mean the pattern of it, the long history, it seems somehow, you know, a folk truth, a radical truth, all these passed-down mythical — ," another of the participants interrupts, "Ahh, your radical mother's mythical cunt!...It's time we junked the whole beastly business, baby, and moved on" (*UBA*, p.233). What one moves on to is another construct, which in turn becomes ossified. The anarchic element that allows Coover's characters some freedom from such constraints is sexuality. Of Hettie it is said that she made them all "forget for a moment that they were dying men" (*UBA*, p.27). Coover's ending in *The Universal Baseball Association, Inc.* is consonant with the one offered in "The Magic Poker": after all the stories woven around them atrophy only the wrought-iron poker and the baseball remain. In "The Magic Poker" Karen "holds it [the poker] up between them a moment, and they both smile to see it. It glistens in the sunshine, a handsome souvenir of a beautiful day" (*Pricksongs*, p.44). In *The Universal Baseball Association, Inc.* "Damon holds the baseball up between them. It is hard and white and alive in the sun" (*UBA*, p.242). These objects serve as foundations upon which have grown rigidified structures, both aesthetic and philosophical, which Coover undermines.

It is with *The Public Burning* that Coover undertakes to assault notions of the state, self, and literature on a monumental level. This novel has been derided by a number of reviewers such as Robert Towers in *The New York Review of Books*. For Towers the novel is a display of protracted carping and spleen. However, when it is read as a radical redefinition of the historial novel, *The Public Burning* is an exciting venture. Ihab Hassan's injunction in *Paracriticisms* to withstand the subjugation or assimilation of the new is apposite here:

> Reaction to the new has its own reasons that reason seldom acknowledges. It also has its rhetoric of dismissal. a. The Fad — "It's a passing fashion, frivolous; if we ignore it now, it will quietly go away."...b. The Old Story — "It's been done before, there's nothing new in it; you can find it in Euripides, Sterne or Whitman."...c. The Safe Version — "Yes, it seems

61

new, but in the same genre, I prefer Duchamp; he really did it better."... d. The Newspeak of Art — "The avant-garde is just the new academicism." (*Paracriticisms*, pp. 41–42)

Some stories already cited by Apple and Barthelme as well as those by Curtis White in *Heretical Songs* and novels such as Doctorow's *Ragtime* and Walter Abish's HOW GERMAN IS IT: WIE DEUTSCH IST ES, as well as *The Public Burning* arguably constitute a distinctive genre: historical fiction differentiated from a more traditional historical fiction by its parodic and metafictive characteristics. Whereas traditional historical fiction incorporates historical details to provide verisimilitude or the texture of a particular period and/or locale, the new historical fiction seeks to deconstruct the historical context, to reveal it as a construct, as artifice. Of Doctorow's purpose in *Ragtime*, Barbara Foley writes, "he is utilizing the reader's encyclopedic knowledge that a historical Freud, Jung, Goldman, and Nesbit did in fact exist in order to pose an open challenge to the reader's preconceived notions about what historical 'truth' actually is."[37] This is in contradistinction to Georg Lukacs' position in *The Historical Novel*: "Detail...is only a means for achieving...historical faithfulness"[38] and characters "in their psychology and destiny always represent social trends and historical forces."[39]

Although J. Hollowell's *Fact and Fiction: The New Journalism and the Nonfiction Novel* and Zavarzadeh's *The Mythopoeic Reality* attest to critical interest in contemporary historical fiction, their focus has been primarily on writers such as Truman Capote and Norman Mailer whose perspectives differ from those of Coover, Barthelme, and the other writers of metafiction. The work of Capote and Mailer is less of a challenge to constituted reality than it is an acceptance of or a repugnance to the absurdity of that reality. Zavarzadeh, to be sure, hints of a yoking of both approaches when he writes, "The nonfiction novelist's arrangement of facts is not endorsive (authenticating) but mythopoeic: it reveals the disorienting fictiveness inherent in facts."[40] Nevertheless, Zavarzadeh's emphasis devolves mainly on the fictiveness inherent in facts rather than on the myths that give rise to those facts; on the bizarre quality of reality in the contemporary world rather than on the ideology or doxa (a term Barthes is fond of using for a phrase, attitude, or cliché dear to a society) which might account for the bizarreness. Events are transcribed by Capote, Mailer, and others such as Hunter Thompson and Andy Warhol because the events themselves are fantastical and novelistic. Zavarzadeh cites, for instance, what he calls the empirical irony in a remark made to Mr. Clutter of *In Cold Blood* and Holcomb, Kansas on the day he is murdered: "Why, Herb, you're a young man, forty-eight. And from the looks of you, from what the medical reports tell us, we're likely to have you around a couple of weeks more."[41] Uncle Sam's sodomizing of Richard Nixon in the "Epilogue" of *The Public Burning* is clearly remote from the incidents Mas'ud Zavarzadeh culls from such works as *In Cold Blood* or Mailer's *The Armies of the Night: History as a Novel, The Novel as History* or Andy Warhol's *a*. The writers woven by Zavarzadeh into a generic framework balk, according to him, at presenting any hint of metaphysics. He lauds them for undermining the precepts of the total-izing novel in which the authors present their narrative correlatives, and render their private readings of the world. Their works succeed because of the way they resolve what Zavarzadeh calls the tension between the centrifugal energies of reality and the centripetal forces of fiction: the fiction approximates the condition of reality.

Zavarzadeh's formulation is inapplicable to a writer such as Coover despite Coover's rejection of the totalizing novel, which he effects by parodying the totalizing novel. The *raison d'être* of his fiction is to diminish the tension between reality and fiction in order to unearth the ideologies or constructs that mould historical events; in this way he apprehends the real and the fictive as analogous. A comparison of scenes from Mailer's *Miami and the Siege of Chicago* and *The Public Burning* provides a sense of the divergence of emphases in the two schools. Both scenes involve elephants defecating, a motif which rarely appears in American literature. Mailer reports the arrival of a baby elephant, a gift to Richard Nixon from the people of Anaheim, California, at Miami's International Airport for the Republican Convention:

> ...the day took on surreal and elegant proportions...the elephant crate was unloaded, hoisted on a fork lift off the carrier, brought near the trailer and opened, everyone gave a cheer to Ana who came out nervously from her crate, but with a definite sense of style. She took a quick look at the still photographers surrounding her, and the larger movie cameras to which certain humans were obviously connected, stepped on the still-wet steaming runway, threw a droll red-eye at her handler, dropped a small turd to x the spot of her liberation from the crate...then did a good Republican handstand, trunk curved as graciously as a pinkie off a teacup.[42]

Complete with cheerleaders called the Nixonettes and the phalanx of media people, the event, a typical if inane political occurrence, reported with a modicum of embellishment (for example, the trope at the end of the quotation), takes on surreal dimensions.

The elephant shit excerpt from *The Public Burning*, Coover's own extravagant invention, provides more frenzied activity. Led by Betty Crocker onto the Times Square stage constructed for the Rosenberg executions, the members of the United States Supreme Court, with the exception of Justice William O. Douglas, make their way towards the podium and then their seats only to lose their footing in the elephant droppings. These were also produced by a Republican elephant which is part of the vast carnival of political and cultural afflatus surrounding the stagecrafted electrocution. "[F]eet flying, robes fluttering, arms outflung and grabbing at space — WHACK! SPLAT! Ker-SMASH! When the shit clears, the six Justices are seen, exhausted and blinded by the muck, floundering aimlessly on their hands and knees."[43] Indiana University cheerleaders shouting "He's our man," and a roll call of the entire Senate are only part of the hyperbolic scene in a hyperbolic novel in which Richard Nixon and Ethel Rosenberg kiss passionately in the Sing Sing death cell. Yet the novel also contains a vast, even encyclopaedic array of facts and data, which Coover has assembled about the period. In his review of the novel Robert Towers writes, "Though one is aware that a show of erudition about a recent decade can be rather easily worked up by reading back issues of *Time* and the *Times*, the *inclusiveness* of Coover's recreation is astonishing."[44] In addition, of course, Coover uses historical personages and develops their characters from his exhaustive research; Nixon's Whittier College days, his and Ethel Rosenberg's adolescent thespian achievements and many other verifiable events are woven into *The Public Burning*. The juxtaposition of factual occurrences, which give the novel its historical authenticity, and fictive extrapolations, which give it its fantastical quality, is meant to elucidate the sensibility of a nation which responded to the Rosenbergs in as rabid a manner as it did.

The focuses of Mailer and Coover in the above passages as well as elsewhere are antithetical: Mailer delineates praxis, Coover the ideology which accounts for praxis. For Mailer the unfolding of events is itself significant; significant for Coover is what shapes this process, the cultural context within which the events unfold. Lukacs' notion of historical faithfulness posits an assimilation of invented detail into a valid historical framework; in *The Public Burning* the reverse is true.

Instead of adhering to the doxa "truth is stranger than fiction,"

Coover and those grouped with him above seek to reveal the ideology which determines truth and to render it understandable. As Robbe-Grillet echoing Barthes has written, this ideology is elusive because it "is established order which is masked as natural order....In order to function correctly in society, ideology needs to be masked to hide its artificiality and needs as well to be continuous, since ideology can only function as a totality."[45] For Coover the ideology, which shaped the America of the late forties and early fifties and has contributed to the enduring American spirit, is a pernicious one. In *The Public Burning* an Entertainment Committee chaired by Cecil B. DeMille to flesh out the electrocution extravaganza does not seem out of place beside some of the actual events and the journalistic pronouncements made during the Rosenberg trial. Coover cites, for instance, some remarks found in Westbrook Pegler's column: "The only sensible and courageous way to deal with Communists in our midst...is to make membership in Communist organizations or covert subsidies a capital offense and shoot or otherwise put to death all persons convicted of such!" (*PB*, p. 16).

Rather than writing totalizing novels in which they foist their metaphysic on what might be regarded as an aleatory world, Coover and the other metafictionists examine the metaphysical and ideological dimensions of American society and history. All the actions and values of American culture are seen as reflective of its prevailing ethos. The perspective is akin to that of the members of the Frankfurt School who rigorously examined the significance of all the forms of popular culture; it was, I think, Max Horkheimer who pithily articulated the semiotical perspective in the following way: it's not that chewing gum undermines metaphysics but that it *is* metaphysics — this is what must be made clear. Most pertinent, though, to the perspective of the new historical fiction is that developed by Barthes, Jacques Derrida, and Foucault. It is not merely that what have been called their structuralist and post-structuralist theories are *de rigueur* in critical circles. It is rather that the thrust of these writers is to denaturalize both cultural and linguistic signs, to demythify the ideological fabric of both world and text. For Barthes, the semiotician, the seminal problem requires that one "'recognize signs wherever they are; that is to say, not to mistake signs for natural phenomena and to proclaim them rather than conceal them.'"[46] In *Système de la mode* and *Mythologies* Barthes undertakes to do just that to the world of fashion and to other aspects of what is called "the real world" such as wrestling, dining, and shopping. By personifying *Time* as the National Poet Laureate,

Uncle Sam as the quintessential pioneering up-beat American spirit, and the Phantom as all that is xenophobically un-American, Coover provides a semiological dissection of American culture, denaturalizing the mythology that constitutes America collectively and individually. A whole chapter, for instance, examines the impact of *The New York Times* on its readers. Also, the structure of *The Public Burning*, in which wide-ranging chapters omnisciently narrating American and international reaction to and preparation for the executions alternate with Richard Nixon's first person narrative, produces the denaturalizing of public and private mythologies.

In "The Blue Guide" Barthes examines the myths propagated by travel books, namely that the stylized approaches to and definitions of nations or regions yield rigidified visions of various peoples. "We find again here this disease of thinking in essences, which is at the bottom of every bourgeois mythology of man" (Barthes, p.75). Uncle Sam's force in *The Public Burning* comes from his demotic, demagogic rants about the idealized vision of America so tantalizingly eulogized in Nick's peroration at the end of *The Great Gatsby* or in Cooper's panegyrics to an uncorrupted continent scattered throughout *Leatherstocking Tales*. This mythology inspired many of the encomia to America, such as Irving Howe's, that are cited in the introductory chapter. It is encapsulated in many of Uncle Sam's speeches such as the following one:

> let us anny-mate and encourage each other — whoo-PEE! — and show the whole world that a Freeman, contendin' for Liberty on his own ground, can out-run, out-dance, out-jump, chaw more tabacky and spit less, out-drink, out-holler, out-finagle and out-lick any yaller, brown, red, black, or white thing in the shape of humanity that's ever set his onfortunate kickers on Yankee soil! (*PB*, p.8)

Much of *The Public Burning* gives ironic vent to the speech that has created Americans' vision of themselves as living in a country predestined to fashion a Utopia. In the novel, Coover writes of "America's gradual unveiling as the New Athens, New Rome, and New Jerusalem all in one..." (*PB*, p.9). He cites a work by S.D. Baldwin which is hardly ideologically neutral; *Armageddon: or the Overthrow of Romanism and Monarchy; the Existence of the United States Foretold in the Bible, Its Future Greatness; Invasion by Allied Europe; Annihilation of Monarchy; Expansion into the Millenial Republic, and Its Dominion over the Whole World* and works like it help to shape the American sensibility, to fix its essence, and to produce susceptibility to the McCarthyite witch-hunts and the consequent immolation of the Rosenbergs. It is apt that Coover has Uncle Sam sodomize Richard Nixon in an inauguration undergone by other Presidents before him; American values are in that way transmitted to each generation's leaders. It is also appropriate that Richard Nixon feels Julius Rosenberg's mistake was to deny the American essence. He muses:

> In a very real sense, Julius Rosenberg was going to the electric chair because he went to City College of New York and joined the American Students Union when he was sixteen. If he'd come to Whittier instead and joined my Square Shooters, worn slouch sweaters and open collars with the rest of us, it wouldn't be happening. Simple as that. (*PB*, pp. 185-86)

Richard Nixon is one of the myth consumers Barthes defines in the theoretical essay that concludes *Mythologies*. He understands a semiological system as a system of facts, reading myth not as a construct but rather as a part of nature. The tenacity with which he accepts reality is heroic, especially in the amorous death cell scene with Ethel in which he relates proudly to her that he helped initiate a Negro into his fraternity; furthermore, he "personally opened up Whittier College to on-campus dances and championed the end of compulsory chapel!" (*PB*, p. 432). Uncomprehending of the Derridean universe in which there is the acceptance of a world of signs which is non-teleological and has neither truth, nor origin, Nixon again and again utters doxa. As a character in a novel, Nixon is unaware of his clichéd existence. *Roland Barthes*, by contrast, contains a portrait or construct of Barthes that chafes against the limitations of character creation. The epigraph, "It must all be considered as if spoken by a character in a novel,"[47] serves to undermine the certitude with which Barthes presents himself and by extension the certitude with which all autobiographers present themselves and all biographers present others as rounded characters. *Roland Barthes* vitiates traditional notions of graspable and definitive characters and identities. Only the conventions of text and world permit such illusions. In the germane fragment — a comfortable mode for him — entitled "Lucidity," Barthes states,

> What I write about myself is never *the last word:* the more "sincere" I am, the more interpretable I am, under the eye of

other examples than those of the old authors, who believed they were required to submit themselves to but one law: *authenticity*....My texts are disjointed, no one of them caps any other; the latter is nothing but a *further* text, the last of the series, not the ultimate in meaning: *text upon text*, which never illuminates anything. (*RB*, p. 120)

Rigidified modes of thinking and writing yield only pre-ordained conclusions and bolster the naturalizing of mythology. Barthes is a structuralist insofar as he accepts Lévi-Strauss's notion that one of man's fundamental functions is to structure experience, to impose form on reality. As a semioticist he wishes to decipher and clarify the processes by which we structure and to resist the assimilative forms or myths which mask those processes. Barthes proffers literature as a language that resists myths as much as is possible — "Doom of the essay, compared to the novel: doomed to *authenticity*—to the preclusion of quotation marks" (*RB*, p. 89).

The Public Burning, certainly the most transfixing of the new historical fictions, provides a similar archaeological restoration and demystification of the bourgeois ideology. It contains the most sustained and energized assault in Coover's canon on the structures masked as recalcitrant reality. Its apparent differences from Coover's other works stem from its focus on one specific historical period, in fact on three days in 1953; indeed, there is an unrelenting and microscopic dissection of that short time span. Yet its strength is the depth and scope of its demythifying processes. If, as Barthes avers, the natural is a legality, Coover's unmasking of what was apparently natural in the period in question is his coup. Encyclopaedically, he deconstructs the Rosenberg executions to reveal the ideology and doxa that contributed to them. For example, the chapter "Pilgrimage to *The New York Times*" analyses the impact of *The Times* on the populace, presenting the newspaper as appearing commandment-like on slabs of stone in the city's centre. The language Coover uses is redolent of ritual and religion: the readers are worshippers who have broken fast before the monument. As he does in *The Universal Baseball Association, Inc*. Coover recites in McLuhanesque fashion the way a newspaper assimilates what he calls the daily detritus of the human enterprise:

The government of Argentina orders the price of theatre tickets cut by 25% and the President of the United States is given a large toy model of Smokey Bear. The execution of an unemployed housepainter in Berlin takes shape beside the report that a new collection of wall coverings and shower curtains offers a variety of choices to homemakers who wish to decorate the bathroom: BATH WALLPAPERS / ARE EASY TO CLEAN. (*PB*, p. 190)

Seemingly a stock assessment of the format of a newspaper, which integrates the monumental and the trivial, the description gives way to an extrapolation of the paper's ideological significance. *The Times* is not ideologically neutral, and this regardless of its editorializing: for Coover the recording of events in *The Times*'s format is itself ideological. Despite the diffuse and heterogeneous items it reports, it assimilates them into its habitual format. Entropy and anarchy are denied no matter how entropic or anarchistic the data assembled. "[E]ven this extravagant accretion of data suggests a system, even mere hypotyposis projects a metaphysic" (*PB*, p. 191). Coover renders this judgement in a chapter which recreates *The Times*'s frenetic quality. Athletes and show business people of the period, actual obituaries and gossip items — all suffuse the chapter to provide the reader of the chapter as difficult a task of semiotics as the reader of the tablets who "discovering in them hints of the terrible abysses beyond the tablets" (*PB*, p. 196) is nonetheless imprisoned by the paper's insistent verbiage.

Before being incarcerated Julius Rosenberg presents himself before *The Times*'s shrine and is outraged that advertisements for pink cigarettes (suitable for weddings) and reports of lost parakeets are being featured concurrently with vital world news. He perceives the paper's narcotizing function: "nothing living ever appears here at all, only presumptions, newly fleshed out from day to day, keeping intact that vast, intricate, yet static tableau — *The New York Times*'s finest creation — within which a reasonable and orderly picture of life can unfold. No matter how crazy it is" (*PB*, p. 192). Only Julius and especially Ethel (as well as the non-appearing Justice William O. Douglas who ordered the temporary and futile stay of execution for the Rosenbergs and to whom *The Public Burning* is dedicated) appear to be impervious to the ideological onslaught. This onslaught includes not only *The Times* but also *Time*, *Life*, and effectively the entire range of American media and media personages, the whole phalanx of which seems to answer Coover's roll-call in the novel.

The one who has ingested the prevailing ideology most fully is, of course, Richard Nixon. Of the Rosenbergs' life style, he muses,

> they hung out with friends who lived pretty unconventional
> lives. People Pat and I wouldn't even know how to talk to.
> They seemed to live without any structure, without any roots,
> yet they never went anywhere! I'd grown up across the river
> from the Mexican ghetto of Jim Town, so I knew what one
> looked like, but I couldn't imagine *living* in a ghetto. I couldn't
> understand why people didn't just move out and go some-
> where else. Lack of imagination or something. (*PB*, p. 128)

Richard Nixon's middle-American imagination is most evident in his
momentous confrontation with Ethel Rosenberg in the death cell at
Sing Sing. Impelled by his desire to eradicate the obstinacy with which
Ethel rejects American values, he relates to her in an almost heroic
manner. Kissing and fondling her he envisions an idyllic world: "My
head was full of poems and justice and unbelievable end runs. I saw
millions of people running to embrace me" (*PB*, p. 439). However,
when he wishes to translate his passion into speech or action, his
imagination produces only clichéd responses. His monologue in the
chapter in question is replete with stylized poses, as well as fragments
from plays and films. Stagecraft supplants genuineness. On meeting
her he composes himself "as though expecting to be photographed. Or
rather, expecting nothing of the sort, but recalling from other photo-
graphs that such a pose suggested alertness and vitality and clarity of
vision" (*PB*, p. 430). Throughout the meeting he strives to remember
and articulate lines from plays, which would encapsulate powerful
"natural" feelings. At one point, when he bursts out crying, the
genuineness provokes him to exclaim inwardly that he has produced
"real" tears. Yet even when he seeks to say goodbye before being
caught with his pants down (literally), he can only grope for lines from
The Valiant, a play in which Ethel had starred while in school. That he
succeeds in redeeming himself in the eyes of mainstream Americans
when it turns out he has been pushed onto the Times Square stage with
"I AM A SCAMP" written in lipstick on his posterior is a tribute to his
stage-managing abilities. His speech to the assembled throng about
America being caught with its collective pants down, a sardonic
acknowledgement of his effective "Checkers" speech, produces a
massive symbolic display of nationalistic pants-dropping. The fervour
evokes the hysteria surrounding the McCarthy era as dignitaries and
general populace alike are forced to show support for the nation in this

way. Stagecraft, games, plays, the paraphernalia of *homo ludens*, man the game player, are used liberally by Coover in the novel. The allusions to *The Valiant* and other plays, the staging of the electrocution in Times Square, phraseology replete with sports metaphors such as "Fuchs to Gold to Greenglass to Rosenberg — quadruple play!" and "The Phantom has a score of 800,000,000 to Uncle Sam's 540,000,000" embody Coover's vision of people possessed by a rigidified sensibility that imperils their ability to respond intuitively and think imaginatively. It allows them to explore the world only in terms of a scoreboard, one featuring "us" against "them."

By selecting actual historical events as the stuff of his fiction in *The Public Burning* Coover contributes a blurring of the boundary between fact and fiction. Even James Fenimore Cooper, though, was suspicious of historical authenticity. In *The Last of the Mohicans* he writes,

> as history, like love, is so apt to surround her heroes with an atmosphere of imaginary brightness, it is probable that Louis de Saint Veran will be viewed by posterity only as the gallant defender of his country, while his cruel apathy on the shores of the Oswego and the Horican will be forgotten. Deeply regretting this weakness on the part of a sister muse, we shall at once retire from her sacred precincts, within the proper limits of our own humble vocation.[48]

Cooper's coyness about the sacred precincts of history, however, has long since been abandoned. None of the metafictionists regards history as sacrosanct. In *The Sot-Weed Factor*, Barth upbraids the muse of history more directly and racily: "Be it remembered...that we all invent our pasts, more or less, as we go along, at the dictates of Whim and Interest....This Clio was already a scarred and crafty trollop when the Author found her."[49] Thus, the kind of historical fiction written by Coover and others should be seen as one attempt, among many contemporary, metafictive endeavours, to denaturalize the facts, forms, or disciplines by which Americans authenticate and understand existence.

   Much of contemporary American literature, then, can be seen to be semiotical in nature, an attempt to read American culture as a system of signs, to denaturalize that culture, its inhabitants, and its literature.

71

A major reason for this preoccupation is the peculiarly emphatic and colonizing character of the American sensibility, which is combatted in terms of the structures it has spawned. Gass and Coover are only two writers for whom the American monolith is pernicious, is a cathectic icon, which needs to be devalued. Certainly Gass and Coover are, respectively, metafiction's most flamboyant and devastating theoretician and practitioner. Their iconoclasm, though, must not be seen as aberrant; rather it emanates from a situation in which American artists see their countrymen as suffused in an ideology, suffocated by a country and its specious solidity. Their relationship with America and its social and literary products is clearly adversarial. There are no colloquia convened in the United States such as there are in Canada through which they utter or would want to utter patriotic proclamations. Nationalism had coalesced around an identity long before they arrived on the scene. They do not see their role as vital to sustaining that identity, again as by contrast Canadian writers appear to do; theirs is the subversive task of denying the legitimacy of such an enterprise. That is why they can be understood as postmodernist in spirit. The conventions of prose fiction and the trappings of selfhood, regarded as allies in solidifying a sense of culture, are combatted as fervently as are nationalistic sentiments. Anarchism, ontological and lexical distrust — these are markedly political attributes of Gass and Coover and give their writing its feisty, obstreperous quality. Not only are they unable to grant their nation ontological security, but they are also aware of the deleterious consequences of doing so.

Robert Kroetsch:
Figure of Rapprochement

"Kroetsch's novels seem to be American rather than Canadian."
—Frances W. Kaye,
"The 49th Parallel and the 98th Meridian:
Some Lines for Thought," *Mosaic*

ROBERT KROETSCH provides an ideal and unique bridge between Canadian and American sensibilities and literary practices. Born in Western Canada he has written fiction which is laden with Prairie dramas, Prairie characters, Prairie winters. However, Kroetsch does not write out of a localized perspective alone. In addition to attending the Iowa Writers' Workshop, Kroetsch taught for seventeen years at the State University of New York at Binghamton. While there he was, as has been mentioned in Chapter One, a founding co-editor of *boundary 2: A Journal of Postmodern Literature*. (In the spring of 1976, *boundary 2* convened a symposium on postmodern literary theory.) Presently he teaches at the University of Manitoba where he actively pursues critical studies in the relationship of Canadian and American literatures. Not only does he acknowledge that Gass and Hawkes are two writers whom he likes, but Kroetsch also reveals that he is as restive as they are with the limits of traditional fiction: "Some of the conventions of fiction control too much our way of seeing the world. It starts to get interesting when you take those conventions and both use them and work against them."[1] Moreover, Kroetsch is acutely aware that the concerns of Canadian writers differ from those of American writers, for the most part because the orientation of the two countries compels such divergent tendencies. In one of his earlier articles he articulates the American-Canadian difference in the following way: "In America they ask: who am I? Am I by nature violent? Am I basically anti-intellectual? Am I condemned to go on destroying westward?

Canadians do not ask *who* they are. They ask, rather, *if* they are."[2] Even more pertinent is the following statement Kroetsch made in another interview, a comment transcribed by Peter Thomas in his insightful book, *Robert Kroetsch*, which is devoted to Kroetsch's poetry and fiction:

> "There is a communal language which one is responsible to. I think the Canadian writer's sense of responsibility to that voice makes him quite different from an American writer quite often. You get a sense almost of submission to that voice in a lot of Canadian writing. I think in the Prairies right now there is a great deal of concern about hearing that voice. I get uneasy about that surrender to it."[3]

As Thomas makes abundantly clear Kroetsch's work contends with that voice in complex ways, both giving vent to it and undermining it.

Before examining more closely Kroetsch's engagement with the Canadian identity and its subsumption in contemporary fiction, it should be noted that Kroetsch is not the only writer uneasy with the unmitigated surrender to his country's voice. In an interview with Geoff Hancock in *Canadian Fiction Magazine*, Leon Rooke bluntly assesses the state of the short story in Canada as follows:

> Rooke: There is too much sameness in Canadian short fiction. Not enough risks taken....Too many readers — critics too, I guess — saying I don't want, you have given me exactly what I wanted. Not enough love of the big surprise.
>
> Hancock: Do you mean vitality in the form of structure, innovation, language, exploring extremes of character?
>
> Rooke: You bet.[4]

One critic who has also been vociferous in agitating for an other than conservative perspective towards prose fiction is, again as was mentioned in Chapter One, George Bowering. Characterizing modern fiction as ontological and postmodern as epistemological, Bowering also bluntly assaults Canadian fiction for being too preoccupied with voice, which is an accoutrement of the self. In other words Bowering's quarrel with contemporary Canadian fiction is that its acceptance of the staples of prose fiction bespeaks modernism rather than post-modernism. In a recent anthology of short fiction called *Fiction of Contemporary Canada* he seeks to rectify that bias by, first, publishing stories that are experimental in nature and, second, directing the reader to their postmodern qualities. He writes in his introduction that those devotees of an avant-garde literature might deduce that what he presents is a collection of only slightly postmodern pieces. All the writers featured reveal a loss of faith in the realistic story. All, though, also betray a diffidence insofar as the radical revamping of the parameters of prose fiction are concerned.

There are on the periphery of the Canadian literary scene a number of works which may be seen to be in the metafictive mode. Audrey Thomas' *Blown Figures*, Jack Hodgins' *The Invention of the World*, Daphne Marlatt's *The Story, She Said*, Keith Harrison's *Dead Ends*, Martin Myers' *The Assignment*, Ray Smith's *Cape Breton Is the Thought Control Centre of Canada*, Robert Allen's *The Hawryliw Process*, and David Young's *Incognito: A Collection* are a few works which have affinities with that burgeoning American school. Myers' *The Assignment* taunts those readers who in Gass's words demand paper passion. Like John Barth's short story, "Lost in the Funhouse," it depends in part on the interplay of traditional narrative and unsettling authorial intervention for its metafictive effect. Barth chides his readers for being "dogged uninsultable print-oriented bastards";[5] *The Assignment* challenges its readers' notions of fiction in a similarly confrontational manner. In a chapter entitled "Off-Camera Voice" (the cinematic motif is a strong anti-narrative force in the novel), Myers introduces a normative voice which querulously upbraids the writer for toying with him and with the staples of the novel. The voice states,

> When I read, I like questions answered. Mysteries should have solutions. Stories should have endings.... Time is running out in this less than monumental oeuvre and I feel it behooves its creator to pull up his socks and tuck in his loose ends. Having sucked me into his verbal vortex and carried me along this far, he has a responsibility to me surely....After all is said and done, the reader (as any book club can tell you) is the most important thing in any piece of writing.[6]

Parrying the expectations of this hypothetical reader, Myers eschews linear narrative and comprehensive resolutions; instead, he indulges in some Joycean play with form by employing different techniques in different chapters. With "Zoom," "Pan," "Sound Track," and other cinematic devices as his chapter headings, Myers creates a montage of

75

perspectives to suit his cinematic terms. The effect created is similar to that of a director who does not record sequential reality with his camera, but who, by cutting, splicing, and editing, creates his own filmed reality. In "Roll Titles," the penultimate chapter, Myers presents the reader with a catalogue of headlines reminiscent of Barthelme's experiments in *Snow White*. One of those titles is "A NOVEL ASSIGNMENT" which alludes to Spiegel's attempt to carry out his quest or assignment and Myers' attempt to fulfil his own novel assignment — the writing of a novel, one which employs cinematic structural principles. Rather than ending with a fade-out on the characters, Myers chooses to present formal devices in a chapter entitled "Out Takes," which recapitulates various directorial stances and techniques that he adapted or could have adapted to his own authorial purposes.

Less effective than the structural dexterity and Nabokovian wordplay, although containing the Borgesian awareness that reality is a construct, is *The Assignment*'s content. The novel contains the tale of an amnesiac philosophy professor whose reaction to quotidian reality is to build another character for himself, one with purpose, intrigue, and cause-and-effect logic. When Gunnarson is found to have assumed the identity of a shabby junkman named Spiegel, he is committed to the Reality Resumption Institute where he is to be rehabilitated by a Dr. Plassibeau. Myers' message, a Pynchonesque one, is clear (simplistically so): reality is a placebo. In the place of reality is a less complex Tristero system, a committee with a Chief Assigning Officer who assigns the main character to carry out mystically important assignments. The assignments confer meaning on his life, allow him to discern order. Seeing life as a riddle to be solved or as a labyrinth to be escaped implies the shaping of an otherwise amorphous existence into a teleologically-oriented one. In his Spiegel phase Gunnarson muses: "Is someone playing games with me? Games. There it is again. Is it a game? Wait. Games. Rules. Follow the rules. Is there a connection? What is it? And what is the game? Who are the players? What are the rules? Spiegel, you should be worrying. Look at all the puzzles you've got to solve" (Myers, p. 142). Spiegel, however, is never permitted to solve the puzzles; as his name implies he can only mirror the confusion around him. "When there were assignments, it [the world] all seemed to have some point, to be going somewhere, even if it never quite got there. But now..." (Myers, p. 302). His junkman's pursuit carried him, to give life to a bad but apt pun, near to a w.a.s.t.e. system; he embarks on a shadowily motivated quest to retain the baby, Ling, for himself and his low-life friends, and to thwart the attempts of the capitalist, Jones, and his network of influential friends to secure the child. Yet the workings of that system remain closed to him. Despite this, he remains unconvinced by Plassibeau's reality and opts for his Gunnarson identity, his real identity and the domestic and vocational life associated with it, only arbitrarily and on April Fool's day, no less. His perception of the arbitrary or illusory nature of reality remains the one revealed in an earlier conversation with Plassibeau. To the question, whether Gunnarson invented his Spiegel-world, Gunnarson replies, "You mean, is it a figment of my imagination? Invention?...I can only tell you that if it is invention, so are you, so is the institute, so is everything" (Myers, p.347).

Patent invention is the bench-mark of Ray Smith, a relatively unknown and obsessively metafictive writer. Smith's *Cape Breton Is the Thought Control Centre of Canada*, in part a parody of the search for an answer to Frye's question, where is here?, is closest in construction to Barthelme's collage-like *Snow White*. Moreover, the stories emphasize technique and authorial manipulation more prominently than any other Canadian fictions. Smith, in fact, allies himself with experimental writers rather than those writers who utilize traditional plots, characters, and, anathema to Smith, Jamesian point-of-view. In an essay on his own work entitled "Dinosaur," Smith, much like Virginia Woolf who parodied the style of Edwardian novelists in "Mr. Bennett and Mrs. Brown," writes a mock scene from a non-existent novel to emphasize the dated quality of that kind of approach. He calls it the bone of a dinosaur and vitiates traditional notions of linearity and consistent perspective. Engagement with serious thematics by a distanced author is rejected by Smith; instead he sees himself writing speculative fiction: "Generally ironic in tone. Aesthetic in approach; which means, I suppose, an indirect approach to the many social and political problems of the world around us....Spec fic doesn't ignore the world, but approaches it indirectly. The telling point is that...[it has] pretty much rejected the whole creaking apparatus of the Walter-Carol psychological-realism (or whatever it's called) form of writing."[7] Smith goes on to show his awareness of the writers who practise his spec fic. The names reveal his fiction's affinities with metafiction: "Some big dogs in speculative fiction: Jorge Luis Borges, Vladimir Nabokov....Prominent younger dogs: Thomas Pynchon, John Barth, Donald Barthelme, Richard Brautigan."[8]

While Smith's stories might seem either derivative or formulaic to those who have a good deal of exposure to the writers Smith catalogues, they are, nonetheless, a signal achievement in a literary climate inimical to their acceptance. The first story, "Colours," is a parody of the search for meaning in and out of fiction. With Barthelme-like languor (his first sentence, "Port is the well-spring of anecdote," evoking Barthelme's marvellous "Self-regard is rooted in breakfast"), Smith presents five vignettes in which a character, named Gerard but otherwise undescribed, phrases the portentous question, what is important in your life?, in essentially trivial terms to five people. That he does not find an answer does not daunt Gerard whose musings bring the story to a close: "He wanted sleep because at noon he was to meet a woman named Culver who might or might not have had a great-grandfather with a middle name of Jonathan. Or was it Nasturtium? Or Bicycle? Ah well, the details did not matter. In the end there was only the search and, with luck, the pattern. It sure made you think. Gerard yawned."[9] The yawn recapitulates Smith's summation of the whole plot-oriented, realistic tradition.

The title story, "Cape Breton Is the Thought Control Centre of Canada," the most delightful one in the collection, provides variations on the theme of independence and national identity, showing the arbitrariness and strain of such concerns. There is no plot line and the characters who do appear, such as the Polish count and two nameless lovers, do not seem to be integrated. Yet all the scenes deal in some way or other with Canada's sense of itself. Some especially anti-American vignettes treat the matter directly. Others, such as the sections relating to Poland, provide the reader with analogous situations concerning nationalism. Still others, notably the lovers' scenes, undermine the theme either by ignoring it or by placing it on a domestic level.

Of the other stories, "Passion" is an ironic commentary on the archetypally passionate relationship of Heathcliff and Catherine; "A Cynical Tale" parodies the suspense-spy-sex intrigue genre; "Raphael Anachronic" contains a Barthelme-like, fictional portrait of Raphael, transplanted into various modern contexts such as airplanes, wars, and hippie communes. Although *Cape Breton Is the Thought Control Centre of Canada* has an abundance of verbal and technical ingenuity, it unfortunately too visibly labours to ape the prominent younger dogs. Nonetheless, despite the possibly ersatz nature of Smith's pieces, they constitute an attempt to engage prose fiction in a manner vital in other parts of the world but mostly neglected in Canada.

In addition to Smith, Myers, and a few other Canadian writers of metafiction who find themselves exploring the same literary terrain as

John Hawkes, William Gass, Donald Barthelme, and others, there is another group of Canadian writers who have primarily written poetry, but whose forays into fiction have had an anti-realistic focus. In 1974 David McFadden published *The Great Canadian Sonnet*, a forgettable, rambling novel ("a little novel(?) why?, sure it's a novel")[10] spun out of his free associating. More impressively John Riddell and bpNichol, better known as concrete poets, attempted to translate their concern with the anti-transparent, anti-referential qualities of language into the medium of prose fiction. In a collection of his short fictions entitled *Criss-Cross: A Text Book of Modern Composition*, John Riddell offers as one of the epigraphs a passage from Susan Sontag's *Against Interpretation* in which she inveighs against what she calls "the inadequate dogmas of 19th century realism" which, she asserts, have rendered the novel unfit to engage a distinctively contemporary sensibility. Music, the plastic arts, and poetry are seen by Sontag as having broken with tradition to explore incisively what is a differently constituted world. By means of collages, comic strip stories, and protracted concrete poems, Riddell assaults the conventions of narrative. His more orthodox fictions, in visual terms at least, are also provocative; they are Borgesian parables that undermine, in a fashion similar to the stories of the metafictionists, notions of verisimilitude. "The Novel" emphasizes the fictive, the constructed quality of character both in and out of fiction; it concerns a character reading a novel called *The Novel*, which is both by and about him. When the novel's pages are scattered by a draft from the air conditioning, his consort gathers as many of the pages as she can and turns to give them to him: "But he was gone. 'Oh well,' she sighed. She gathered together as many of the pages as she could find. She began to reassemble them, and decided to hope for the best."[11] Extreme consciousness of the process of writing fiction (the way Barth's "Author" contributes to Barth's fictions); central placement of the conventions of fiction and the artist's handling of his materials (the way the magician in Robert Coover's "The Hat Act" showily produces his epiphanic wonders); also, emphasis on the contrived nature of reality (the way Kurt Vonnegut labels the detritus of American industry and ideology a bad fiction): these tenets of metafiction are given nascent form in *Criss-Cross*. More stream-of-consciousness than Nabokovian pattern, bpNichol's *Journal* nonetheless originates in the perspective, essential to the modern writer, that writing is difficult, that language is no longer the serviceable medium which transcribes reality: "maybe there are stories make sense maybe there's

a point you can start from mother where it all ties together the untying
oh I do shift plots or points of view stepping in & out of people who
are not real to me."[12]

Despite the foregoing works, the novels that have found a more congenial and touted reception in Canada are less formally innovative works
such as those by Margaret Atwood, Robertson Davies, Margaret
Laurence, Mordecai Richler, and Marian Engel. Instead of providing
and sustaining a context within which experimentation might flourish,
such works as Smith's and Thomas' appear as anomalies, less salient
products of an important genre. This is where Kroetsch's work is especially relevant; it is so because, if you will, he incorporates the
concerns both of traditional and avant-garde camps. Unrelentingly
ironic, he recognizes demands for voice and identity, for a cultural
framework, but he cannot capitulate to system, stability, or framework. Ann Mandel writes, "Kroetsch proposes a radical uninvention
of Canada's past, a decomposition of all systems of language which
threaten to define him and his literature, an unlearning of myth,
metaphor, and tradition, an uninvention of the world and an
uncreation of self."[13] Mandel's "*un*'s" link up with contemporary
criticism's "*de*'s." She is alert to Kroetsch's unmaking and deconstruction of national and ontological verities.

Although Kroetsch belongs in the postmodernist camp, it is not his
modus operandi to vitiate heedlessly the staples of prose fiction. His is
not a formalist's dismissal of the ontological status of state and self or
of the transparent properties of language as are the novelistic and critical directions of Gass and Coover. Aware of the greater sense of story
and landscape that is a dimension of Canadian fiction, Kroetsch does
not abandon them for the kinds of play indulged in by Smith in *Cape
Breton Is the Thought Control Centre of Canada*. Although he resists
surrendering to the Canadian voice, and with it a messianic dissemination of "here," Kroetsch depends on the differences between Canadian
and American voices for a good many of his techniques and devices as
well as for many of his insights. In an early interview with Laurence,
he states clearly that his Canadian experience has shaped his fiction
writing: He tells her that because they are western Canadians, they are
involved in making a new literature out of a new experience.[14] Such
sentiments are prominently featured in other interviews. "So much of
our prose," he told Donald Cameron, "— and maybe our poetry too, I
would say — is the stuff of daylight....American literature is very

much a night literature...."[15] In that interview he also says, "We become fascinated with problems of equilibrium. Americans are interested in expansion. This difference has to have an effect on our literature, on our language."[16]

Kroetsch, then, mediates between a dissemination of the Canadian identity and a retreat from it, between a desire to reflect distinctively Canadian modalities in his prose and a nervousness about being swallowed or stifled by those very entities. It is no wonder that he revealed to Russell Brown that "I sometimes think I have a sense of irony which threatens to destroy me."[17] Despite his leeriness of the ironic sensibility, Kroetsch realizes it is an attractive mode for one who juggles two antithetical national identities and their attendant aesthetics. It also appeals to one who is sensitive to the special qualities of self and state, but who also finds himself unable either to voice or even to accept the inherent truth of those entities in an unmitigated way. Irony precludes the prophetic or messianic voice; rather it encourages iconoclasm, irreverence. National and personal characteristics are never permitted to solidify, to acquire wholehearted assent.

The ironic consciousness of Kroetsch intrudes in another interview when he says to Geoff Hancock, "I guess I admire Margaret Laurence for daring to invent a kingdom, because I'd like to do that; and all the while I have this scepticism, that works against the ideas of both community and self: reality resisting design..." (Hancock, p.38). Certainly, Kroetsch's reluctance to give unbridled voice to community and self is a far less antagonistic stance, a less overtly political gesture than Gass's or Coover's. They, as was explored at length in the preceding chapters, must confront a solidly constructed and ensconced edifice that has for some time gloried in its sense of self, making greedy, deadly history along the way. No such monolith or reified set of values confronts Kroetsch in anorectic Canada. However, Kroetsch cannot accede to the role of builder, of shaper, one which, as Jay Cantor has deduced, is nurtured in "a time of high talk; in later ages the language seems too unironic, the speech of patriotic pageants."[18] In the words of Wallace Stevens, which Cantor quotes, "The whole race is a poet that writes down / The eccentric propositions of its fate."[19] Such is the lure of incipience, of an inchoate country struggling to create its myths, its voice, its identity. Thus, Grey Owl is such an alluring figure for Kroetsch because he created himself anew, divesting himself of a European legacy to redefine himself. *Gone Indian* which chronicles the climactic moments in the life of an ersatz Grey Owl figure, constitutes an ironic rewriting of that saga. What Cantor calls the revolutionary moment in which national character coalesces and all inhabitants gain poetic redolence by helping to effect that character is too much high talk for the ironic Kroetsch. Although he does not rail against a country's rigidified definition of itself, he does betray a scepticism toward any such monument or constructive activity.

Although his critical vocabulary incorporates a term such as "deconstruction" and reveals a dissatisfaction with realism, Kroetsch's deployment of language reflects a moderate attitude to the language of the regime, the false documents towards which Robert Coover and Gass direct so much vitriol. Kroetsch has expressed that dissatisfaction with the neutral or transparent handling of language which, he feels, is endemic in Canadian fiction: "What intrigues me is the idea of 'foregrounding' as they say. Foregrounding the language itself.... Too many Canadian writers treat it like a heap of fresh bear shit" (Hancock, p. 38). Yet in his fiction he keeps in balance the stories of Western Canada and the epistemological uncertainty behind those stories. In *The Words of My Roaring*, for instance, Johnnie Backstrom is both abashed by and driven towards the utterances of his campaign speeches. The novel begins with Old Murdoch speechifying stumping his district bartering promises for votes. At the novel's end Backstrom is reconciled with and substituted for Murdoch as he rides through the countryside towards Coulee Hill and an apologetic election speech that would seal his victory. Kroetsch's disruptive, anti-teleological sense of language is modified by the country that has only begun to give credence to its own voice, its own speech acts.

Of Gabriel García Marquez, Kroetsch says, "He nips at the heels of realism and makes the old cow dance" (Hancock, p. 38). Rather than an outright dismissal of narrative, Kroetsch engages in similar legerdemain. If, as Jay Cantor claims, "[t]he language of mimesis assumes a separation between words and things and a self that uses the language,"[20] Kroetsch finds himself able to use that language only ironically. His engagement with postmodernism, specifically the writings of Derrida, has in all likelihood germinated the scepticism he feels vis-à-vis language as a transparent medium and the self as autonomous. For Derrida, "a subject who would supposedly be the absolute origin of his own discourse and would supposedly construct it 'out of nothing,' 'out of whole cloth,' would be creator of the *verbe*, the *verbe* itself."[21] Such a logos-centred theory of language is rejected by Kroetsch as it is by Derrida. Nonetheless, his fiction shows a sympathy for those who strain to inhabit such a universe. Derrida, after

Lévi-Strauss, calls such a figure an engineer, one who does not recognize the inability, the impossibility, of removing oneself from a system of signs in order to control and employ it. "The engineer...should be the one to construct the totality of his language, syntax and lexicon" (Derrida, p.256). The engineer is contrasted with the *bricoleur* who accepts that such a yearning is a myth: "the odds are," writes Derrida, "that the engineer is a myth produced by the *bricoleur*" (Derrida, p.256). In other words, whereas the *bricoleur* discounts transcendence, the engineer does not.

The latter, of course, is a far more amenable figure for the definition of a country and the reshaping of a self within that state. The epigraph Kroetsch uses for *Gone Indian* is from Frederick Jackson Turner's "The Significance of the Frontier in American History": "For a moment, at the frontier, the bonds of custom are broken and unrestraint is triumphant."[22] Such is the lure of Grey Owl as symbol. He aspires to being an engineer as his contemporary avatar, Sadness, does. Kroetsch, then, does not treat his engineer characters hostilely as do Coover and Gass, because the denizens of Kroetsch's country have not engineered their country's identity in any calcified way.

In *Robert Kroetsch*, Thomas seizes pertinently on Kroetsch's penchant for probing what Thomas calls the ficticity of selfhood and state and of the role of language in the making and unmaking of both. He relates Kroetsch's strategies directly to these concerns.

> Kroetsch's habit of deconstruction applies as much to regional or national models as to literary structures. In a crucial sense, Alberta will always remain "Alberta" for him, and Canada a silence into which voice must be projected from an elusive and solitary necessity....[T]he interrelationship between the given symbols of the prairie and Canadian land and the strategies of language, of narrative itself, is explored with great vigour and ironic complexity....Perhaps it is...[in *The Studhorse Man*] that Kroetsch's conviction that a Canadian Eden can only be ironic is best expressed....(Thomas, pp.120-22)

For Thomas, Kroetsch's postmodernism coalesces around just such an awareness, the making and unmaking of identities. *Robert Kroetsch* develops how all of the novels, as well as the collections of poetry, work through that concern. Thomas finds in Kroetsch's poem, "F.P. Grove: The Finding," a paradigm for his avant-garde activities. Kroetsch's precept, "fiction makes us real," finds its model in Grove, who, like Grey Owl, reconstructed himself anew in Canada. Even more intricately Thomas discovers in the poem the duality, coyote self and taught man, or the free, elusive, regenerative being, and the more circumscribed being caught in history. That the former inevitably succumbs to the latter increases the complexity of the dialectic. Such a kinetic situation also leads to the destabilizing of the concepts of self and state and the tenuous relationship of word and world. It is this motif which Thomas examines in all Kroetsch's work to date.

Although Thomas' discussion is a fine one, a further extrapolation of three of Kroetsch's novels, namely *Gone Indian* and *The Studhorse Man*, as well as the recently written *Alibi*, can be developed with the limits of this study in mind. Because *Gone Indian* is an ironic rewriting of Archie Belaney's recreation of himself as Grey Owl, because it straddles the Canadian-American border with Jeremy Sadness having fled from Manhattan via the State University of New York at Binghamton to the Canadian northland, because it contains Jeremy's aborted attempts at his dissertation, and, finally, because it mixes academic discourse with oral Indian stories — for these reasons *Gone Indian* raises all the questions about national and individual identities with which Coover, Gass, and other contemporary American writers grapple. *Gone Indian* also serves to situate Kroetsch more precisely as the figure of *rapprochement*, a position which snippets from earlier interviews only suggested.

Of the novel in question, Thomas writes the following: "The invented self in a fictive world is most completely exemplified by Jeremy Sadness in *Gone Indian*" (Thomas, p. 4). Jeremy's compulsion is "to 'be Grey Owl'" (Thomas, p. 69), and for Kroetsch the metamorphosis of Archie Belaney most typifies, after Grove's, the quest for a dreamed identity. Jeremy is first glimpsed in Professor Madham's anecdotal account of his having lost his suitcase, a precipitous divesting of his identity. Moreover, the first words heard directly from Jeremy (the chapters alternate between Madham's wry assessments of Jeremy's doings and Jeremy's tapes to Professor Madham) are that he could not, there at Customs minus his own baggage, remember his name. "For a fatal moment my stumbling, ossified, PhD-seeking mind was a clean sheet" (*GI*, p. 7). To rid himself of his identity is to remove himself from the prison-house of language as Kroetsch's juxtaposition posits. To become Grey Owl is to free himself from the welter of words which paralyses him throughout the novel. Dissertation topics recur in his mind and on his notepads to taunt him about the lexical playfield he wishes to escape. In addition, the women with whom he engages in sex while a graduate student are connected in one way or another with libraries, literature, or the printed word; there was, for instance, "Miss Petcock who worked in the library of the State University of New York at Binghamton, a young lady who wore short skirts, very short skirts, and who, one morning, showing me how to use a microfilm reader in the basement of the library, yielded, even there, up against the reader that she had only then switched on..." (*GI*, p. 115). Also, of course, Jeremy's wife, Carol, worked in the xerox room at the university in order to support him while he worked towards his doctorate.

The clash in terms of language in *Gone Indian* is between a world written out painstakingly and pedantically and an oral pre-literate culture freed of the fetters of dissertations and other examples of scholarly dissection. Jeremy's mentor, Professor Madham, given the task of explaining everything to Jill Sunderman, tries to make sense of Jeremy's actions by interspersing his own explanatory prose with excerpts from Jeremy's tapes. The contrast is clearly between a print-oriented approach and an approach that seeks to flee or evade such a mode. As Thomas defines it, Madham "represents the whole post-lapsarian intellectual tradition and its structures....Jeremy seeks to return to source, to deny the Fall by decreation" (Thomas, p. 70). In much of the novel Kroetsch indulges in something seldom seen in his other works, a caricature of the university ambit that he knows so well. Indeed, Jeremy's nominal quest to the West is to land an academic job at the University of Alberta. From his conversation with the chairman, a Professor Balding, at that institution, to his encounters with an office-mate and fellow graduate student whose "idea of a benefit [is] a lifetime subscription to PMLA," the witty Jeremy reveals Kroetsch's caustic sense of the academic milieu. Jeremy's dalliances with his shapely students show that Kroetsch suffers from an ennui, a jaded despair about the edifices of language and learning. This despair is particularly well shown by the desecration of his office during one such dalliance: "What is a destructive passion, Mr. Sadness? she inquired. My office looked like a barbershop after, there were pubic hairs scattered from my *Norton Anthology* through *Anatomy of Criticism* to my notes on Bishop Berkeley (thus I refute my Bishop)" (*GI*, pp. 45–46).

His anodyne is to be sundered by Jill and finally Bea Sunderman from a stereotyped and restricted culture. Jeremy's sadness necessitates that he use his trip to Alberta to search for a more elemental, atavistic milieu than the urban Eastern one in which he was born and had always lived. Finally, he scorns and rejects his wife, his major professor and advisor, and all the trappings of the civilized world represented by his hot-house academic and literary training and potential career. Asked early in the novel if he is looking for someone, he answers, "No.... Nothing. Yes, I am looking for nothing. The primal darkness. The purest light. For the first word. For the voice that spoke the first word. The inventor of zero" (*GI*, p. 22). Despite a Herculean effort in his first race on snowshoes, Jeremy Sadness spends the remainder of the novel metaphorically running backwards, running away from the accretions of civilization accompanied by the wry interpolations of his wife's paramour, Mark Madham. Having learned to drive in the parking lots of SUNY Binghamton, Jeremy progresses to the point at which he drives Bea Sunderman to her home, apocalyptically and aptly called "Worlds End." Later, he and she abscond more literally to that place with their final escape.

Between those deliberately placed events, the last concluding the novel, Jeremy undertakes his regression or divestiture. While loitering in Edmonton before the supposed interview for an academic position, Jeremy spontaneously orders Jill to follow a pick-up truck driven by an Indian and containing dog sleigh and dogs. That odyssey returns him to Notikeewin where he is to judge the winter festival's queen. Accosting the Indian, he shouts, "Did you ever hear of Grey Owl?" and "Did you ever run into Grey Owl?" (*GI*, p. 65). Soon after, he enters a snowshoeing race having never worn snowshoes; but he remembers "the drawings in one of Grey Owl's books, the pencilled notation: 'snowshoe lifts in front only, hanging by toe bridle'" (*GI*, pp. 81–82). Throwing off clothing which impedes him he doggedly snowshoes attempting to discover the "Nothing... The first word. The inventor of zero." Even after he crosses the finish line he continues on until he is tackled by someone: "I was fighting to free myself. Because the magpie was escaping, was flying off, out into space. But someone, shouting, had caught me, was flinging me down in the snow" (*GI*, p. 88).

Kroetsch's novels are strewn with figures who are in flight, literally and metaphorically, from confinement of all kinds. From Hornyak's madcap driving through *But We Are Exiles* to the ski-jumper in *Gone Indian* who crashes in his attempt to overachieve to Roger Dorck for whom Jeremy substitutes at the carnival, Kroetsch depicts characters who have to be tackled, subdued, brought back to earth as happened to Jeremy. Nevertheless, Jeremy moves indomitably away from the academic-domestic world of Binghamton and its other cloned

86

outposts of culture. Rescued by Mr. and Mrs. Beaver, the Indians whom he had espied in Edmonton, Jeremy is given and dressed in moccasins belonging to the Beavers. This further removes him from the persona he inhabited at the beginning of the novel. Soon after, Jeremy has his dream of absorption into the figure of an Indian, and also into an anti-social Dionysian ecstasy ("He danced himself free...dancing...until the flesh...tore free..." [*GI*, p.101]). Apocalyptically, "[h]e dreamed the scalping of Edmonton. The last city north. The Gateway" (*GI*, p.103). Also he imagines his run backwards from civilization completed — "He might have been in a cave, the last Stone Age hunter at the end of the Great Hunt, dreaming his final prey. Thirty thousand years from Europe..." (*GI*, p.103). Insistently comic as well as ironic, Kroetsch has Jeremy experience a final metamorphosis into a buffalo.

Regardless of the bathetic denouement, Jeremy's *rite de passage* is a meaningful one and culminates, again comically but vitally, in a mock death scene which marks his progression from Ph.D. candidate to "BUFFALO WOMAN," which Jeremy writes on a pad while acting as the judge of the Winter Festival's Beauty Pageant. After his presiding at the Festival and before sleeping in the coffin in Backstrom's funeral parlour, Jeremy, who responds to Jill Sunderman's dictum, "We will dance until dawn," thinks, "I wanted to dance, let me tell you. Just once in my goddamned fucked-up book-spent life, I wanted to dance clean through the night: damn the unwritten papers. Damn the forthcoming exam" (*GI*, p.123). Not long after his comic entombment, Jeremy, who emulates Robert Sunderman and other Kroetsch escapees, arrives at "Worlds End" and carries off Bea Sunderman; in Professor Madham's words, "they rode away seeking NOTHING. They sought NOTHING. They would FLEE everything" (*GI*, p.156). Their snowmobile is found on the cowcatcher of a locomotive with which it had collided on a trestle bridge; the tape recorder is discovered hanging from one of the pieces of timber in the middle of the bridge. The bodies of Jeremy and Bea, however, are not found. Jeremy thus attains liberation from his modern self.

Gone Indian is a witty, raucous novel that contains a keen insight into the lure of redefining or recreating a self. Like Coover's or Gass's characters, Jeremy Sadness experiences a revulsion against the conventional self he has been slated to embody. As Thomas points out, Jeremy's rejection of that self and his awareness of the constructed quality of that identity are paramount even at the beginning of the novel when Jeremy "first encounters a transvestite, in the customs changing room at the airport ('Maybe the cock and balls are fake too, I don't know.')" (*GI*, p. 8), and when he himself escapes from custody ("I shall bravely, recklessly, escape from this suffocating dungeon: DISGUISED AS MYSELF" [*GI*, p. 11]). For this reason Thomas labels Kroetsch a postmodernist, given that the world of the postmodernist "'reality' exists between a half-acknowledged, half-recollected belief in the possibility of radical reconstruction of selfhood, through the descent to ground, silence, or the leap into chaos, and a tradition of deterministic structures and absolute 'models'" (Thomas, p. 76). Also this defines Kroetsch's trenchant irony, his play with postmodern notions of the self as construct as well as more securely grounded notions of the self. Madham's academic mode of understanding and structuring the world and Jeremy's atavistic mode of fleeing it are compared, undermined, and inverted. Each cancels the other; neither subsumes nor dominates the other.

Kroetsch's attitude to language and to the state is similarly complex. There is a strong attraction on the part of Jeremy and other Kroetsch protagonists to be Adamic poets, naming freely and unfettered by tradition. There is also the lure, especially pronounced in Jeremy, to flee the limits of a print-oriented milieu altogether. Yet *Gone Indian* has two narrators, one committed to that culture, the other trying to escape it: the storyteller, who is part of an ancient, oral culture, and the writer, who is part of a more contemporary culture.

The Studhorse Man contains a similar dichotomy, two main characters as opposed as are Madham and Sadness. Demeter Proudfoot, the narrator, is a writer and virgin, who seeks to write Hazard Lepage, the eponymous studhorse man of the title, into a story which will immortalize and mythify the man. Demeter calls the work "this portentous volume," and strives to provide an explanatory account similar to Madham's. Hazard Lepage's quest is far less abstract than Jeremy's. He travels the land to offer his horse, Poseidon, as a stud. He searches for the mare which will maintain Poseidon's noble lineage through its foal. Insofar as Demeter is concerned, he seeks to transform himself into Hazard, calling himself "D. Proudfoot, Studhorse Man." He gives himself this name after he rescues Poseidon, whom he takes to the mansion Lepage inhabited, and after he almost consummates his relationship with Martha Proudfoot, Lepage's fiancée of thirteen years. Ironically named after the fertility goddess, Demeter, by assuming Lepage's identity as the supremely phallic hero and then, by writing Lepage's story, a more dispassionate activity, tries the two ploys that were attempted by Sadness and Madham respectively.

88

Lepage, like Jeremy, pursues a more unabashedly primitive and carnal course. Living for Poseidon's fruitful ejaculations as well as his own ("Hazard touched his bearded face to her flesh and nipped at her thigh....I swear before God and man that he whinnied"),[23] Hazard seeks to maintain a self unmoulded by civilization. Once again Kroetsch dualistically presents him as both bound, in this case to Proudfoot's prose or to the page, and freed only ultimately in death. Language is a constraining element, providing Proudfoot the means of capturing Lepage's life but also fixing it there. In his bathtub Demeter places one of his three-by-five cards on his penis,

> and pirates we sail here together in my bathtub, our cargo the leather-bound books and the yellowing scribblers, the crumbling newspaper clippings and the envelopes with their canceled stamps and the packs of note-cards that make up the booty of our daring.
> What have we captured? what saved?[24]

These questions echo throughout Kroetsch's fiction — they bespeak the evasiveness of reality from language, the tenuous quality of character as it is caught or created in art. Indeed, Thomas finds that in *The Studhorse Man*, "Kroetsch parodies the tradition of formal realism and its aspiration to 'objectivity' in several ways" (Thomas, p. 61).

Thomas also astutely traces the novel's engagement with the Canadian state. "By using the Canadian national motto, 'From sea to sea,' as a structural pun on the meaning of *mare* / mare" (Thomas, p. 51), by having the participants touched and in some cases damaged by the First World War, by giving Lepage an Arcadian lineage so that he "is not at home in either of the 'two nations'" (Thomas, p. 53), by presenting Louis Riel as rejecting a plea of insanity, and, finally, by citing the English influence and impact on buildings and statues in the Canadian West, Kroetsch incorporates the question of the Canadian identity into his novel. For Thomas, "the essential movement throughout is from a historical to a fictive Canada" (Thomas, p. 51). As in *Gone Indian*, Kroetsch provides a sense of the state that is dualistic: the attraction of defining a place and the ultimate hollowness of such an activity. Despite the rural or earthy dimensions of both novels, he examines the idea of the state in a sophisticated and complex manner. His achievement has been to

> transform the familiar and dreary trap of the realistic "Prairie novel" (or "Northern" novel for that matter) into a frontier of

fictive possibilities. When he told Margaret Laurence that "the experience of absence is an experience" and "the vacuum idea is wrong" he was raising the flag for a planned escape from the deterministic hell of the garrison mentality....(Thomas, p. 78)

All language, to quote Hayden White in his article on Michel Foucault,[25] is catachresis, in other words, misuse. The "doom in language,"[26] in the lexicon of *Alibi* is that it is all alibi (from the Latin *alius*, other). It occupies an alien place rather than a literal one, at best, possibly a littoral (on which a great deal of the action of *Alibi* takes place). Thus, "[w]e are all exiles" (*Alibi*, p. 151) (cf. Kroetsch's *But We Are Exiles*), displaced most acutely not from central Alberta but from logocentrism, denied the "direct epileptic Word" and "pulsing stelliferous Meaning."

Underpants flesh out this motif in *Alibi*, but are, of course, no substitute for, or rather, are *only* a substitute for the flesh beneath. A less sophisticated postmodernist such as Vonnegut might, in *Breakfast of Champions*, crudely draw underpants and write, "I see England, I see France; I see a little girl's underpants!" mocking the semiotics of desire before he draws the "wide-open beaver"[27] that itself is only a sign. For Kroetsch, though, the play of language and consummation, word and world, is an intricate one, a Derridean replication of substitutions that always already ensnares man in alibis. Dorf, Kroetsch's protagonist, first encounters panties in profusion when he walks into a laundromat and discovers a woman named Estuary folding them: "and the panties...were splendid too, one pair golden, another lime green, one pair as blue as a noon sky, one pair the color of fire, suggesting beaten bass, filigreed; panties embroidered, emblazoned..." (*Alibi*, pp. 32-33), stacks of them.

Dorf, remember, is an agent for the rich and idiosyncratic Jack Deemer whose passion is collecting esoteric and exotic objects; Dorf hunts, gathers, and secures the various collections. In the novel's present he has been commissioned to locate spas, especially the perfect one. Estuary's name certainly is redolent of the spa, the underground river or source. Estuary needs the medicinal properties of spas for the deformed hand which is the mark of her mortality; so too does Deemer who is aging and it is rumoured ill. Dorf also feels the need for a spiritual anodyne despite his robustness. Dorf enunciates his quest and links Estuary, underpants, and a cure when he thinks, "I connected the panties with Estuary and Estuary with the woman I was looking for and the woman I was looking for with a dream of being healed. I was hurting, I knew that much. We cannot have what we want, and we hurt" (*Alibi*, p.35). While Dorf successfully locates the woman he seeks and while he has little trouble finding the artifacts he searches for, he is less fortunate as far as his health is concerned. In fact, Dorf is ultimately denied healing. Alibis provide no such succour.

Indeed, after finding Julie, the woman he had been looking for, Dorf shares a triolage with her and the dwarfish doctor de Medeiros only to have the underpants motif recur:

> ...I imagined she had on panties, strawberry red, and he took them off, and she still had on panties, the color of mint this time; and I spoke the colors aloud then, spoke aloud the names of these colors.... I imagined he took off another pair, a bitter shade of lime, and still she wore beneath that lime need, against his taking, more panties and more, until he could never find her.... (*Alibi*, pp.128–29)

The doom in language, which frustrates all of Kroetsch's central characters, is here yoked to the underpants; it is in its persistence as a seemingly friable but ultimately unyielding divide that it taunts Dorf, catching him up in a play of signifiers which always keeps covered what it promises to uncover. Language is also a barrier to Julie's "motion, her mouth's silent need" (*Alibi*, p.128), and it provides a contrast with "the delicious scream of her outraged pleasure" (*Alibi*, p.129).

Articulation (from the Latin *articulare*, to divide into joints) troubles Dorf as acutely as it plagues Jeremy. Also, Dorf's atavistic longings are as compelling as are Jeremy's. As Jeremy's desires are embodied in his quest to be Grey Owl, Dorf's longings find their avatar in the smelly woman of the Laspi mudbaths who, along with other women at the spa who seek healing, provides him with his last orgasm, an ecstatic, muddy masturbation in which Dorf sees himself as his own baptismal "fountain." He cries out, "no words, no names, only a pure cry of total joy and total pain" (*Alibi*, p.180). Circumventing language here, Dorf attains an ecstasy free of identity. His full name is William William Dorfen, the patronymic itself a short form of Dorfendorf; the two Williams are double trouble to Dorf who yearns throughout the novel for a unitary, a holistic sense of self and world. He is especially desirous of escaping language's leavings; he even foists one of his given names on a stranger who says he has no name and then takes on the nickname, Billy. Not incidentally Dorf has moved into Billy's shack at the end of *Alibi* trying to live, as it were, namelessly.

It is at Laspi, though, that Dorf is most fully realized. Here, despite the fact that he cannot understand the Greek that is spoken around him, he communicates and communes more freely than he ever had been able to. Of himself and his uncomprehending spa partners he says, "We had a language that whole nations might envy" (*Alibi*, p. 176). Furthermore, he becomes an autochthonous creature, revivified by the mud which he daubs on his body and which is all he wears. "[M]uddily human" (*Alibi*, p. 172), he has divested himself of the modern self with which Jeremy Sadness had sadly to contend. Unlike Jeremy, though, Dorf does not "go" Indian indefinitely. Although Deadman Spring contains the ideal spa with its redemptive estuary, Dorf is not ready to withdraw completely as Jeremy did. He remains, after all, at the end of *Alibi* writing his own alibi, the journal that is the sign of his continuing condition.

Ousted by the smelly woman from his prelinguistic haven, he finds his loss (his being decentred) compounded when he rediscovers Estuary. This time he comes across her in a Greek taverna where she sits only a few chairs away from him, exposing the "hot green flare of her panties" (*Alibi*, p. 183). Immediately his thoughts return to the smelly woman whom he remembers as a hermaphroditic creature, taking on for him wholeness: "she was and she was not language and idea, dream and reality, good and evil, Satan and God" (*Alibi*, p. 184). She represents a pre-articulate, pre-divisive bliss that he had for a short time known in Laspi. Because she possesses the wholeness that Dorf lacks, she is able to transform him figuratively into a hermaphrodite by drawing "invisibly, slowly, with one finger, the pattern of an opening on the top of my head" (*Alibi*, p. 185). Absorbed in this reminiscence Dorf forgets Estuary who has disappeared by the time he thinks to glimpse again her panties.

Underpants are not the only item Dorf catalogues through the course of the novel. Indeed, his job as Deemer's collector has caused him to itemize many things. That vocation is congruent with and as estranging as Jeremy's proposed dissertations. Dorf's taxonomic and structuring enterprises are vain endeavours to order a heterogeneous, articulated world; his order of things is as stylized, rigidifying and hierarchizing as that order delineated in Foucault's ironically titled *The Order of Things*. It is while having sex with Julie in one of Banff's sulphur pools that Dorf first remembers one of his collecting sorties for Deemer. With his phallus tied to his locker key by its wrist cord, Dorf thinks of the locks he purchased from a woman in Connecticut:

her locks, some of them, mounted in doors that were mounted in the middle of a large room, doors that led from nowhere to nowhere, the exquisite complexity of their locks available to any who would look, the secret connivance of figure and letter and sign, available, teasing the eye that would know, confounding the mind with the very unwillingness to hide. (*Alibi*, pp. 14-15)

While ruminating thusly Dorf's phallus (key) is in Julie's vagina (lock) unlocking their desire. Yet that unlocking is juxtaposed to the doors that lead from nowhere to nowhere and to the exquisite complexity of their locks. These are locks that can be picked, which give up their secrets (the secret connivance of figure and letter, and sign). Language, however, is a more intractable medium, with no code that can be deciphered.

Soon after this coupling with Julie, Dorf goes to his hotel room with Karen Strike only to have difficulty with the lock; "[t]he infernal key was worn" (*Alibi*, p. 19). In his shower preliminary to their lovemaking, Dorf discovers that "[t]he words HOT and COLD, it turned out, were on the wrong taps over the deep white tub" (*Alibi*, p. 21). The scalded penis that results from the transposed signifiers renders him temporarily useless as a lover. Unlocking the secrets of language in which man is enmeshed is infinitely more difficult than picking door locks which man has made. As Dorf plangently tells Karen, "People never tell.... That's the way it is. They can't" (*Alibi*, p. 27). In addition, as Dorf broods snidely over his sister's positivism, it occurs to him that "Sylvia regarded herself as the guardian of truth and language, as if there was, somehow, a connection between the two" (*Alibi*, p. 86).

Karen, who resembles Sylvia to the extent that neither of them is undermined by the ineluctable division of words and things, plays Madham to Dorf's Jeremy. A documentary moviemaker whose current work is "on the forgotten history of forgotten spas" (*Alibi*, p. 17), Karen works intransigently to unlock their secrets. Girded with a government grant, she cannot be deterred from making a movie for television or from articulating "The Mechanics of Healing." As Dorf tells the reader in the journal which concludes *Alibi*, it is she who has provided Dorf's story with its veneer of order: "Let Karen put in some headings, some chapter titles to trap the unwary eye and lure the customer; she with her gift for compromise" (*Alibi*, p. 231). Indomitably she makes films and approaches men; "MAKE DO" is the logo she boldly wears on her t-shirt. She insists on her point of view as tenaciously as does Madham his, handling her medium, again, as surely as he does his.

By contrast, Dorf is more vulnerable, this despite his skill as a collector. Karen reports that Deemer compliments Dorf in the following way: "You work in circles, in tangents, in loops, in triangles. But you always get to the center" (*Alibi*, p. 97). In fact, he manages to gather everything Deemer seeks; nonetheless, even the insistent Deemer's taxonomic and acquisitive enterprises (for which Dorf is the agent) cannot dispel for Dorf the thought that there is no centre, no source, nothing outside the system that disperses the system into a coherent pattern. As he waits for Deemer in the perfect spa at Deadman Spring, Dorf thinks, "possibly that emptiness, that absence, that nothing at the center of the cave where water falls from solid rock, is enough, is everything" (*Alibi*, p. 218). There is no logical beginning to or regeneration in any of Dorf's quests for Deemer including the spa assignment, this despite Karen's best efforts at stage managing.

Called "Ecstacy, Extasie, Ekstasis," presumably by Karen, the last chapter promises an ecstasy that despite the apparatuses of a few languages eludes inscription in the text. After the lights fail, those in the spa seek to establish contact by calling each other's names: "we named our strangeness away" (*Alibi*, p. 227), with god-like names, too, such as "Jehovius" and "Wah" (Yahweh) (*Alibi*, p. 227). However, Dorf indicates in his journal that he was violated, sodomized, in the darkened spa. The Adamic naming of the moment is not a transfiguring naming. Articulation remains equivocation. As Dorf queries by Julie's coffin, "And what the hell isn't a message in this world we live in? And what is?" (*Alibi*, p. 199). Julie, like Bea Sunderman, sensed this condition; in a question reminiscent of Dorf's perspective she asked, "We all live by our alibis, don't we, Dorf?" (*Alibi*, p. 125). She also asked significantly, "Is the place of cure a place?" (*Alibi*, p. 124). Her death indicates a refusal to provide alibis.

Calgary, Dorf contends at one point, is a gridded city, the dead of that city resting in "rows and patterns" (*Alibi*, p. 195); in the Greek town, Salonika, he sees "a jumble of shops that sold car parts... sorted now..." (*Alibi*, p. 191). Dorf, who is Deemer the absent redeemer's sorter, senses the futility and sterility of this fundamental human activity. In the last entry we have from his diary, he remembers securing a collection of carved and ceramic horses for his employer. In the collection he finds a book of poetry in which the first poem contains the cry of the osprey, "Gwan-Gwan." The book is a translation as is all language, substitution of sign for sign in a never ending play of signifiers. "Gwan-Gwan," the osprey's sound, though, is what the ospreys he has been observing utter. It is a pre-literate cry that Dorf reveres, one not trapped in the labyrinth, the prison-house of language. Dorf's happiness, here, refers the reader back to his interaction with an octopus on a littoral. The octopus straddles his groin, in a way making love to him. "It was unimaginably cool, a cool poem I later explained...not a study of a poem but the poem itself, finding me" (*Alibi*, p. 153). Dorf's bliss, in the mud, with the octopus, is always an inarticulate, which is to say a non-divisive one. Nonetheless, Dorf's dilemma is not naively solved. Unlike Jeremy Sadness who must get out of the world to preserve his integrity, Dorf writes out his story (history) knowing that it is alibi, catachresis. Trapped in a language that is not an efficacious instrument which can write him out of his malaise, Dorf reveals the scepticism all of Kroetsch's characters feel towards the illusory quality of language as a transparent medium. Only the octopus which disappears perfectly into the sea innocently manifests its language.

For Kroetsch the Canadian possibility involves playing off notions of entrenched state with those of an open frontier, one of infinite possibilities; playing off ideas of solidly defined characters against those of inchoate characters able to redefine themselves in frontier surroundings; playing off a language of the regime, written and acceded to, against a language of freedom, newly minted and untarnished. Whereas Coover, Gass, and other contemporary American writers must expend a good deal of energy and anger attacking the entrenched elements of state, self, and language, it is Kroetsch's fortune to be able to write in a less confrontational situation. His metropolitan Madham and Strike and yearningly atavistic Dorfen and Sadness, his Apollonian Proudfoot and Dionysian Lepage, his documented, factual prose and tall tales, his Prairie realism and myth-laden dramas — all combine to give Kroetsch's fiction the consistently ironic quality he astutely recognizes. In his awareness of the experimentation ongoing in the contemporary novel and in his enjoyment of the storyteller's role, Kroetsch incorporates two sharply differentiated tendencies; in addition, his balancing of contemporary American practices with contemporary Canadian ones makes him a figure of rapprochement. Moreover, his novels are rich and unsettling because they do not subscribe simplistically either to the strident definition of place or person or to the renunciation of it.

Canada: Atwood and Davies

"The true Canadian voice is a mutter."
— Anon.

IF, AS SEEMINGLY every Canadian critic contends, the Canadian identity and Canadian image are too meagrely conceived by those at home and abroad, then the enunciation of a Canadianization program has surely become an important Canadian genre. Diagnoses and prescriptions, assessments and manifestos abound. They have proliferated as virulently as have attacks on the American identity by those writers cited in Chapter Two. Northrop Frye's *The Bush Garden: Essays on the Canadian Imagination*, Atwood's *Survival: A Thematic Guide to Canadian Literature*, Ronald Sutherland's *Second Image: Comparative Studies in Québec/Canadian Literature*, and the collection entitled *Read Canadian: A Book about Canadian Books* edited by Robert Fulford, David Godfrey, and Abraham Rotstein are only some of the major statements that attempt to develop a sense of the country via its primarily literary products. The writers of these books share the presupposition that yoking Canadian nationalism and the Canadian literary enterprise is a salutary, even a valuable, activity.

When Davies writes in "The Canada of Myth and Reality" that "One of the tasks of the Canadian writer is to show Canada to itself,"[1] he does not mean the revelation of a repugnant image, some monstrous reified entity such as Robert Coover and William Gass present. On the contrary, he and the other practitioners of the genre refer to an as yet uncreated, but nascent identity that has a significant and important role to play, namely the fostering of a cohesive and identifiable sense of place. Although Margaret Atwood maintains, in an interview with Graeme Gibson,[2] that she is no politician and therefore eschews hortatory or propagandistic prose, she, too, accepts Davies' premise that to sustain and to nurture her country are far from nugatory or jingoistic purposes. Certainly it is true that she has pursued such ends primarily in her non-fiction, most notably *Survival*,

96

in the interviews she has given, and in the occasional pieces she has been called upon to write. Despite the fact that only the occasional diatribe intrudes and obtrudes in her novels, most prominently in *Surfacing*, her concerns with individuals' identities and their tenuous hold on those identities as well as her handling of the form of fiction indirectly and metaphorically yield a sense that she is committed to establishing a national place as well as an individual person.

Clearly what the works by Frye, Sutherland, Atwood, Fulford, and other nationalistic critics are redolent of is an urgency to establish the significance and congruence of the Canadian experience, to give it the intellectual and cultural testaments which will demarcate place with the specificity and, more important, the unanimity with which Walt Whitman's *Leaves of Grass* and Abraham Lincoln's Gettysburg Address demarcate American history, American progress. "Fifteen Useful Books," an appendix of sorts to *Survival*, "The Ten Best Canadian Books" in *Read Canadian*, and Frye's "Preface to an Uncollected Anthology" (of English Canadian poetry) in *The Bush Garden* attempt emphatically to reveal to the reader, who it is assumed is bereft of an indigenous tradition, that core texts aspiring to the status of Canadian classics have been written, do exist, and need only a broad currency and consensus to provide that solid definition of Canadian culture which, concomitantly, would reduce the notion that this is an ill-defined, inchoate country, devoid of such points of fixity and communion as the Statue of Liberty, Daniel Boone, and *Moby-Dick*.

The germ for *Read Canadian*, Fulford explains, was just such a situation as the above in which a lack of knowledge of Canadian texts by Canadians is displayed. In what is now perhaps a stock anecdote, Fulford tells of a high school English teacher who wanted to engage Canadian literature but who had received no preparation for such a venture in her Canadian university career. Atwood asserts in *Survival* that "the tendency in Canada, at least in high school and university teaching, has been to emphasize the personal and universal but to skip the national or cultural."[3] Davies, too, reminisces about the Canadian cultural void in which he grew up: "My parents were great consumers of periodicals and printed matter [which] crowded into our house from England and the United States every month" (Davies, p. 11). Common motifs and experiences such as those noted above link the overtly nationalistic books. By reiterating the anorectic condition of Canada the writers of such texts hope to rectify if not eradicate that malaise, to extirpate the sense of void or importation which they feel so dominates the cultural life of their country.

Read Canadian was conceived of as a continuing project. A biblio-graphical as well as an analytical text, it surveys works in fields as diverse as Canadian history, Canadian publishing, and drugs. In the essay devoted to modern fiction, W.H. New acknowledges that the dominant mode of recent fiction has been the *Bildungsroman*, the growth-to-maturity novel, most especially as it delineates the develop-ment of women in modern Canadian society. Written in the early 1970s the essay asserts further that realism has given way to a fiction which "more openly admitted the artifice of its technique and as one of its aims held language itself up to contemplation."[4] Nonetheless, with the exception of Dave Godfrey's *The New Ancestors* with its meta-phoric application of Africa's evolutionary situation to Canada's, the works New mentions devolve quite consistently on a traditionally pursued (both thematically and technically) quest for identity.

Read Canadian provides, in a fairly matter-of-fact way, a list of meritorious Canadian works that would fill out one's sense of this nation in all its aspects. It also contains a manifesto that could lead to a rigorous cultivation of Canadian books. Among the tenets of that manifesto, most of which are enumerated in an essay entitled "Publishing in Canada," are the following:

> — If you're a student and someone suggests that you buy and read a U.S. text, check to see if there aren't Canadian books on the same subject and, if there are, unilaterally substitute the Canadian for the American.
> — If you're at a Canadian university, give an inscribed presen-tation copy of *Read Canadian* to every one of your U.S. professors.
> — If you're a writer, always discuss your manuscripts and projects with Canadian-owned firms first and avoid the branch plants.[5]

To read Canadian, it is hypothesized, will be to think Canadian, not as the megalomaniac Uncle Sam in *The Public Burning* thinks American, but with a distinctive voice that Davies in a surprisingly diffident piece has called an unassuming one. Assessing this country as one that is "so wanting in the rich sense of the past — of an individual self-made past — that is the prized possession of other nations" (Davies, p. 14), Davies encourages Canadians to regard themselves as possessors of a voice, albeit one that is not forceful and self-centred. On the contrary, the voice is that of a "secondary character, the hero's friend, the confidant; but the opportunity and heart... is that of one who may be a hero, and a new kind of hero, a hero of conscience and spirit, in the great drama of modern man" (Davies, p. 14). Regardless of the modesty with which the Canadian character is supposed to be formed, there is here an encouraging sense of place and character. One of the ways to nurture that vision, it is maintained, is to read Canadian literature as an extension of Canadian nationalism. Davies writes that "so many Canadians who are eager to bring forth a new spirit seem to think either that we have no past or that it is unworthy of consideration" (Davies, p. 10). To rectify that situation he draws attention to Douglas LePan's 1948 poem, "Coureurs de bois," which yields the image of a "'Wild Hamlet with the features of Horatio,'"[6] the supportive friend from whom Davies generalizes about Canadians.

In *The Bush Garden* Frye offers similar clarification of the sediment of Canadian literature, finding in it the nucleus of a tradition that has been neglected only because it has not been placed in the foreground with the literatures of other countries. He acknowledges the impact of A. J. M. Smith's *Book of Canadian Poetry*, which appeared in 1943, and which, Frye declares, "brought my interest in Canadian poetry into focus and gave it direction. What it did for me it did for a great many others: the Canadian conception of Canadian poetry has been largely formed by Mr. Smith, and in fact it is hardly too much to say that he brought that conception into being."[7] Shoring up the notion of an indigenous literature has as its corollary that indigenous literature's value not intrinsically as literature, but rather extrinsically as a national resource. In his "Conclusion" to the *Literary History of Canada*, Frye contends that Canada has not produced any authors about whom it can be legitimately claimed that they are international in stature, or rather, that they are among the world's major writers. Therefore, "[i]f no Canadian author pulls us away from the Canadian context toward the centre of literary experience itself, then at every point we remain aware of his social and historical setting" (Frye, p. 214). For Frye, then, the literature of Canada has a claim upon its readers only insofar as that literature divulges a sense of place. He even goes so far as to say that Canadian literature "is more significantly studied as a part of Canadian life than as a part of an autonomous world of literature" (Frye, p. 214).

What with Irving Layton having been published in a number of languages, Atwood being fêted in a number of countries, and Frye, himself, having achieved international stature, such a timorous claim might be disputed by some of the more virulent and unapologetic of nationalistic critics. Nonetheless, the *Literary History of Canada* was published in 1965 and despite the fact that fiction as practised by Mordecai Richler, Margaret Laurence, Atwood, and Marian Engel, among others, has flourished, Frye's comments are not atypical of the way many in the country want its literature read. "One theme which runs all through this book is the obvious and unquenchable desire of the Canadian cultural public to identify itself through its literature" (Frye, p. 216).

To realize this yearning has been, Frye relates, a difficult enterprise. Geography undermines the attempt somewhat, he avers. Without a congenial Atlantic seaboard and a sharply etched symbolic port of entry, Canada is not reached as memorably as is the United States: "to enter Canada is a matter of being silently swallowed by an alien continent" (Frye, p. 217). The American Revolution, Canada's two languages and cultures, and the dominance of the United States over Canada are often mitigating features Frye cites which contribute to a meagre image of place. Frye writes that Canada has "developed with the bewilderment of a neglected child" (Frye, p. 221). Consequently, Canadian literature comes to be seen as an anodyne, something to counteract the tendency towards self-effacement and lack of confidence. The vocabulary, itself, of forays such as Frye's and Atwood's is revelatory. Minatory diction, rife in the work of American critics such as Hassan, is non-existent in Canada where diction and tone are encouraging, supportive. The threat is not the country, itself, but rather it is to that country. Literary traditions, those that are rooted in one's own soil, are vital according to Frye in combatting the danger. The writer "needs them most of all when what faces him seems so new as to threaten his identity" (Frye, p. 250).

Seen as a matter of survival, Canada's self-image is examined most poignantly, of course, in Atwood's *Survival*. Atwood asserts forcefully that survival is the dominant Canadian motif just as the dominant American motif is the frontier and the dominant British motif the island mentality. Such subsistence self-imagining has led, she postulates, to victimization, to the recurrence of victims as characters in Canadian literature. Canadian authors, though, are seen to be resistant to such passivity. Atwood places them, in her lexicon, in "Position Four: To be a creative non-victim" (*Survival*, p. 38). This relationship to one's society is not the antagonistic, confrontational one that operates for Gass and Coover in America; rather, it allows the poet or novelist to act as tutor, as the articulator of goals and ideals that a country might espouse. The enemy for Atwood, Frye, and other Canadian literati is clearly not an active, firmly constituted nation. It is, on the contrary, one that has not been fully formed. Concluding her theoretical, introductory chapter to *Survival*, Atwood proffers the following maxim: "Much of our literature is a diagram of what is *not* desired. Knowing what you don't want isn't the same as knowing what you do want, but it helps" (*Survival*, p. 42). If Coover and Gass see their country as a victimizer which needs to be deflated, Atwood sees her country as a victim which needs to be inflated. Much of *Survival* diagnoses the various postures of victimization and rebellion that are adopted vis-à-vis nature, the climate, family, and society. In each case the explicitly hortatory end is to transform positions of victimization, to combat them.

Survival is more interesting as a document about the way Canadian critics develop the context for the reading of Canadian literature than it is an incisive, disinterested look at the works themselves. This is not an infrequent mode of approaching Canadian literature. The supportive role of the book obtrudes at the end of *Survival* when Atwood writes, "Any map is better than no map as long as it's accurate, and knowing your starting points and your frame of reference is better than being suspended in a void. A tradition doesn't necessarily exist to bury you: it can also be used as material for new departures" (*Survival*, p. 246). To carve out and name that tradition has been the Canadian critical legacy. As such it has been impervious to the whole deconstructionist debate that has gripped academia in America. It has also given short shrift to other entrées — Marxist, phenomenological, and Freudian — in favour of, as Davey has assessed, the sociological and more specifically the nationalistic.

When Atwood provides the following peroration she does so with a committed, public bias, calling on Canadians to affirm themselves cohesively and distinctively.

> Even the things we look at demand our participation, and our commitment: if this participation and commitment are given, what can result is a "jail-break," an escape from our old habits of looking at things, and a "re-creation," a new way of seeing, experiencing, and imaging — or imagining — which we ourselves have helped to shape. (*Survival*, p. 246)

Such a program requires the overthrow of foreign definitions, modes inimical to the Canadian character which, Atwood and others feel, has not had the chance to form and flourish.

An examination of the novels of Atwood and Davies reveals no such polemical thrusts as the works studied above adumbrate. Atwood, in fact, has said in a *Malahat Review* interview, "If I wanted to propagate my vision of Canada, I'd be a philosopher. And if I wanted to impose it on everyone, I'd be a politician or a minister."[8] In addition, a wry assessment of nationalistic concerns can occasionally be found in the work of both writers; for example, in Davies' *Leaven of Malice* the young academic, Solly Bridgetower, reacts gloomily to his advisor's bequest of the dramas of Heavysege, an early Canadian writer, as well as of the field of "Canam" literature. Nonetheless, the fiction of both Davies and Atwood reveals a surer sense of place and of person, or, at least in Atwood's case, the struggle to articulate person, than does the fiction of Coover and Gass. Both Canadian writers use language in a largely referential way, providing the verisimilitude that is a staple of realistic fiction and that authenticates the world and the word's relationship to it.

In regard to person, place, and language Atwood and Davies are by no means atypical of contemporary Canadian writers. Probably the only male writer with Davies' stature in Canada is Richler. Richler's novels, though, exploring the urban Jewish milieu and portraying the part-schlemiel, part-bright boy who is the dominant persona of Saul Bellow's and Philip Roth's novels, reflect the North American Jewish situation; consequently, they place less sharply in the foreground the attitudes and techniques that differentiate Canadian from American. In the matriarchal realm of Canadian fiction there are a number of other women writers who have written fiction that examines the territory Atwood's novels cover: a contemporary woman seeking to define herself in opposition to a predominantly patriarchal society. Laurence and Engel are two whose works would qualify. Nonetheless, because Atwood's critical statements have been found to be so germane to Canadian fiction and because her poetry, as well as her fiction, has given her a pre-eminent place in Canadian literature, her oeuvre yields the greatest insight into the situation of the artist in Canada.

Despite the works mentioned in the previous chapter and despite the fine series that Quadrant Editions is producing in a format that occasionally incorporates works that might be suitable for publication by the Fiction Collective, the novels of Atwood and Davies have achieved a reputation that places them in the forefront of Canadian fiction. A diatribe against such a situation is not in order here or elsewhere, for that matter. Nonetheless, Davies' Trollopian, conversational novels and Atwood's two most recent works, *Life Before Man* and *Bodily Harm*, which lack the incisiveness about the search for identity that bolsters her earlier works, do not bear up to the praise lavished upon them. All of Atwood's novels with the possible exception of *Surfacing* lack, for all the terseness and laconic quality of her poetry, the taut structure so frequently found in post-Jamesian fiction. In a conversation with Joyce Carol Oates, Atwood said, "One can only afford 'a thoughtful consideration of technique' when the question of mere existence is no longer a question."[9] Such an assertion contains vital clues for the direction of contemporary fiction in Canada as well as for Atwood's own work. One could argue that the traditional novel with its commitment to character development and to all the limits of social life enmeshes one in a technique that confers meaning on the world. Importantly for practitioners of the genre, this is not seen to be a political, a significance-conferring choice. Rather, the genre is regarded as a vehicle, a medium that is not a message. Also, the realistic novel is regarded as normal, the experimental novel as an aberrant, ephemeral phenomenon. The novel which is replete with Nabokovian erudition and play is dismissed as effete; in its place is a novel with the traditional staples of prose fiction. These act transparently to conduct the reader directly to the dilemmas of character and country.

Thus, whereas Robert Kroetsch handles lineage and genealogy ironically in *Badlands*, Atwood employs them much more univocally in *Life Before Man*. The question of fossilization and of the study of behaviour from it is a motif which can be found in the epigraph taken from Björn Kurtén's *The Age of the Dinosaurs* to *Life Before Man*. Lesje, Nate, and Elizabeth, the three main characters in the novel whose monologues succeed one another's throughout the work, produce the deposits that will come to be known as contemporary man and woman. The fossilization motif also appears in Lesje's daydreams, her disinterested observation of dinosaurs a reflection of the reader's disinterested study of her. "In prehistory there are no men, no other human beings, unless it's the occasional lone watcher like herself, tourist or refugee, hunched in his private fern with his binoculars, minding his own business."[10] Atwood's skill with iterative imagery is as apparent in her fiction — from the food motif in *The Edible Woman* to other imagery in more recent novels — as it is in her poetry. The purpose of such a device is not to call into question the very structures of characters and novelist, as it does in the work of a much less trope-oriented writer such as Kroetsch; rather, it affirms the quest of the character and contributes to the linearity, the teleological direction of the novel.

Despite the disruptions and dislocations, often severe, which are undergone by Atwood's heroines, the form itself remains unshaken and serene. Despite the occasional anguished or angry epithet uttered by the protagonists of *Surfacing* or *Bodily Harm* or *Life Before Man*, the language of Atwood's fiction remains solid, a still useful means of communication; this despite her characters' often desperate search for the sureness that exists beneath their public personae, physical, cultural, or linguistic. In short, the surface of Atwood's novel has not suffered the distortions found in *Omensetter's Luck* or *The Public Burning*. Despite the awareness manifested in her novels that language is often obfuscatory, layering reality rather than revealing it, the language of the novels retains its security. Similarly, the structure of Atwood's novels works relentlessly to confirm the importance and translatability of the deeds of her questing heroines. One gets the sense that although technique is not vital to Atwood's writing of fiction except as a scaffolding upon which to relate the actions of the novels, it is important secondarily, confirming that the question of mere existence can be answered. Even if the heroine of *Surfacing* barely accedes to her humanity at the end of the novel, each of Atwood's protagonists is caught up in a *Bildungsroman* in which a redefinition of self is contemplated if not affirmed.

Language is a cumbersome medium which each main character tries to shirk, to get beneath; so, too, body and name are tested as being false fronts and go through a good many transformations. Nonetheless, Atwood's novels yield a sense of solidity. Of the language in even her most elliptical novel, *Surfacing*, one critic has said, "Even in moments of intense mystical perception, her language is the language of logic. She does not experiment with language, she does not go far enough."[11] Despite the falseness of many social impositions, the characters are revealed to have a core, a nucleus, a self beneath language and social mores. As Rosemary Sullivan has written in "Breaking the Circle," that centre is an atavistic one, a kind of Lawrentian kernel encumbered by the husk of civilization. Of the protagonist in *Surfacing* she writes,

> The heroine rejects the husked and literal layers of contemporary consciousness, and tries to recover an earlier, more primitive mentality. In so doing she enacts a radical myth of renewal: she is plunged into total psychic chaos, which is a gateway to a sacred dimension, a primordial time of beginning. The implications of breaking the circle begin to emerge: anarchy leads us to the mythic theme of rebirth. (Sullivan, p. 36)

Similarly, Marion McAlpine and Joan Foster recapitulate this process in which the refusal of food and language and the lure of anorexia and aphasia become powerful metaphors of divestment, of reversion to the core. Unlike Sylvia Plath and her various protagonists whose release from externally imposed constraints and definitions signals a desire for stasis, for death, Atwood's heroines by such an act cultivate the nucleus that they feel is essentially theirs, the nucleus that will allow them to move surely in the world.

As many critics, including of course Atwood, herself, in *Survival*, have commented, the movement in her novels is not one of succumbing to victimization but of triumphing over it. As Tom Marshall has commented in "Atwood Under and Above Water," "running through her work is the theme of discovering and creating self and country, and this is a major Canadian theme — the positive complement or aftermath of the notorious 'victim' theme."[12] Though far from being an ideologue, Atwood in her fiction reveals characters questing for a stable identity. *The Journals of Susanna Moodie* contains in microcosm the dynamics of Atwood's novelistic questing heroines. In her "Afterword" to the poem sequence Atwood asserts that, like Susanna, "we are all immigrants to this place even if we were born here: the country is too big for anyone to inhabit completely, and in the parts unknown to us we move in fear, exiles and invaders."[13] The indomitable Susanna, though, seeks to define herself and her country. Despite "the gritty window: an unexplored / wilderness of wires" that is the vision granted a resurrected Moodie in the final poem, "A Bus along St. Clair: December," there is an atavist's place — "there is no city; / this is the centre of a forest" (*JSM*, p. 61) — "empty" but with the potential to be reconstituted.

Each of the heroines of Atwood's first three novels is anorectic. Metaphorically, this state represents the refusal to accept the detritus of civilization and of character which has accrued around the individual. Rejection of food and also of language, as well as of communication of the social niceties implies not a nihilistic act but a purgation of all that is not essential. As Susanna Moodie attests,

> Though they buried me in monuments
> of concrete slabs, of cables
> though they mounded a pyramid
> of cold light over my head
> though they said, We will build
> silver paradise with a bulldozer

it shows how little they know
about vanishing: I have
my ways of getting through.

(JSM, p. 60)

Marshall, extrapolating further on what Atwood's heroines renounce, maintains that each is "driven to rebel against what seems to be her fate in a technological, 'Americanized' world, and to psychic break-down and breakthrough."[14]

McAlpine's way of getting through and of preparing to reconstitute herself in *The Edible Woman* is sharply delineated, image, symbol, and story culminating in a rejection of pre-ordained roles for herself as woman and as middle class consumer. Some critics, such as Davey, have objected to the overly neat imagery and the work's perhaps pat symbolic resolution. Regardless, Atwood does carry the food motif through with consistency and wit. Atwood's epigraph is from *The Joy of Cooking* and sets up not only the food imagery, but also the image of a surgeon or mortician at work: "'The surface on which you work (preferably marble), the tools, the ingredients and your fingers should be chilled throughout the operation....'"[15] That operation is performed penultimately in the novel by Marian who makes a cake which does not cool quickly enough. "She took it out of the tin and set it on the clean platter, opened the kitchen window, and stuck it out on the snowy sill" (*EW*, p. 268). Once it has cooled she takes it indoors. "Then she began to operate" (*EW*, p. 269). Her operation has created a monster-surrogate, a repository of all that is reflexive, clichéd, passive, the false being created by others, instead of existentially from within.

The Edible Woman ends light-heartedly with the deflation of the cake as symbol — "So Peter hadn't devoured it after all. As symbol it had definitely failed" (*EW*, p. 271). Nonetheless, its significance before the comic ending is not reduced. When Marian is, upon seeing Peter for their final confrontation, softened to the extent that she wants to reach out and touch him, she is jarred by the following thought:

> But there was something about his shoulders. He must have been sitting with his arms folded. The face on the other side of that head could have belonged to anyone. And they all wore clothes of real cloth and had real bodies: those in the newspapers, those still unknown, waiting for their chance to aim from the upstairs window; you passed them on the streets every day. It was easy to see him as normal and safe in the

afternoon, but that didn't alter things. The price of this version of reality was testing the other one. (*EW*, p. 271)

This is a far from comic vision of entrapment; it pictures, instead, a macabre mission of the body-snatchers, people whose aim is surgically to master, to capture. Marian discovers the sham that is inherent in this version of reality and which is forced upon others, especially women.

Marian McAlpine, her name suggesting both the waspish core of Canada, especially bourgeois Toronto, and the solidity of alpine mountains, begins her growth to maturity with a vaguely uneasy sense of the patriarchal world in which she lives and works, but with a quiescent sense of the rightness of that world. At Seymour Surveys she works at a middle management position, figuratively and literally: "On the floor above are the executives and the psychologists — referred to as the men upstairs, since they are all men — who arrange things with the clients..." (*EW*, p. 19). Moreover, her job involves a sex-stereotyped milieu — "our department deals primarily with housewives" (*EW*, p. 20). Also, she is surrounded by women who have been assimilated there; office virgins, getting married and settling down: such is the ambience in which she works. The first glimpse of Marian as a surveyor involves Moose Beer and its stock pitch to men: *Any real man, on a real man's holiday — hunting, fishing or just plain old-fashioned relaxing — needs a beer with a healthy, hearty taste, a deep-down manly flavour* (*EW*, p. 26). Atwood's swipe at sexist advertising would be jejune were it not for the following facts: stereotypes especially in beer advertising have only moderated somewhat; Marian's passivity and acquiescence in the face of Peter's cancellation of their date immediately after her having heard the advertisement.

Nascent, though, in Marian is that feeling of inauthenticity, dissolution, or insubstantiality which permeates Atwood's poems. "This Is a Photograph of Me," the first poem of *The Circle Game*, reveals the speaker submerged, devalued:

> I am in the lake, in the center
> of the picture, just under the surface
> It is difficult to say where
> precisely, or to say
> how large or small I am.[16]

Diminution and vulnerability are caused by imprisonment as in *Power Politics* in which one of the men of whom Peter is a precursor is described as a kind of prison guard:

Put down the target of me
you guard inside your binoculars,
in turn I will surrender[17]

Thus, it is no surprise that there are incipiently in Marian at the beginning of the novel feelings akin to those of the woman in the poem, "This Is a Photograph of Me"; as she leaves work she describes herself walking as "almost like moving underwater" (*EW*, p. 29). Despite such ennui Marian remains a simpleton, consciously content with her situation. When Ainsley tells her she has decided to have a child, Marian reacts with, "'You mean you're going to get married?' I asked, thinking of Trigger's misfortune" (*EW*, p. 39). Marian can only juxtapose what Peter has told her of his friend Trigger's impending marriage and would-be enslavement with Ainsley's situation, heedless of the sex roles which supposedly dispense men into the greedy, marriage-seeking arms of women. Nonetheless, Marian begins to balk subconsciously, to feel the lack of a core, of a self; thus her dream in which she sees herself as amorphous:

> The alarm clock startled me out of a dream in which I had looked down and seen my feet beginning to dissolve, like melting jelly, and had put on a pair of rubber boots just in time only to find that the ends of my fingers were turning transparent. I had started towards the mirror to see what was happening to my face, but at that point I woke up. (*EW*, p. 43)

Marian's anorectic condition ensues. It stems from an attempt to find the kernel, the nucleus of self. Her sense of ontological security can emanate only from a pared-down self, one that has purged the dross or the externally conditioned. To make the metaphorical leap from the refusal of food to the renunciation of alien cultural strains is perhaps too gross a movement. *The Edible Woman* works exclusively on an individual rather than on a national level; however, each of Atwood's heroines (indeed, all of Atwood's work) eddies around notions of autonomy and violation of that autonomy. In many instances a sexist, patriarchal world violates a woman's integrity or undermines her definition of self; in other instances a colonizing, imperialist American force constrains Canadians' integrity and undermines their definition of self. The two, moreover, are yoked in *Survival*, in the victor/victim theme Atwood articulates. If *The Edible*

Woman emphasizes the individual, feminist rejection of control, as part of Atwood's oeuvre it relates to the broader, cultural issue.

Marian's anorexia, though, does have specific and personal causes. Peter's threatening, absorbing dimensions begin to impinge on her more and more acutely as the novel progresses. A whimsical run after an evening drink turns into a chase in which she sees herself as threatened: "All at once it was no longer a game. The blunt tank-shape was threatening. It was threatening that Peter had not given chase on foot but had enclosed himself in the armour of the car..." (*EW*, p. 73). Soon after a reconciliation and removal to a friend's apartment, Marian's accelerating sense of diminishment propels her to seek refuge in a cramped space between the bed and the wall. The scene deteriorates into a comic one in which Marian remains undiscovered for some time, then finds that she is stuck under the bed. Despite the comic elements, though, Marian's situation can be compared to Esther Greenwood's in Sylvia Plath's *The Bell Jar*. When Esther crawls into a womb-like space and then takes an overdose of sleeping pills, the imagery of this action and the attendant discovery and resuscitation confirm that she seeks to divest herself of her old self so that she can be born again as a whole, integrated person. Marian's precipitous actions, though not as cataclysmic, reveal her dissatisfaction with the person she perceives herself to be.

Although her reasonableness forestalls her descent into madness via anorexia, it cannot contain the trauma interminably. Whereas the first third of the novel is told through Marian's largely lucid and sure voice, the point-of-view shifts for Part Two in which Marian is perceived from a more external perspective, the language remaining controlled while the protagonist flounders. Peter's link with the surgeon or mortician is dramatized in Marian's thoughts when his touch is felt to be possessive, "as if he was trying to memorize her. It was when she would begin feeling that she was on a doctor's examination table that she would take hold of his hand to make him stop" (*EW*, p. 149). Finally, she experiences even more vividly Peter as predator. At a party he has thrown, Peter takes her picture, only to be regarded as a hunter in doing so: "he raised the camera and aimed it at her; his mouth opened in a snarl of teeth" (*EW*, p. 244). Escaping for a final time she imagines Peter

> tracing, following, stalking her through the crisp empty streets as he had stalked his guests in the living room, waiting for the exact moment. The dark intent marksman with his aiming eye

had been there all the time, hidden by the other layers, waiting for her at the dead centre: a homicidal maniac with a lethal weapon in his hands. (*EW*, pp. 249-50)

Such a hyperbolic perspective abates quite quickly and the novel ends with Marian's first-person narration and her appetite restored to her. Regardless, the problem of victimization and lack of identity is paramount to Atwood. Whether the victimization is as deadly as Marian McAlpine or the narrator of *Surfacing* or Joan Foster of *Lady Oracle* or Rennie Wilford of *Bodily Harm* imagines, the toll it takes is real enough. Atwood's epigraph to *Bodily Harm* is from John Berger's *Ways of Seeing* and reads: "A man's presence suggests what he is capable of doing to you or for you. By contrast, a woman's presence...defines what can and cannot be done to her."[18] Although the threats to Marian are not literally as severe as she imagines, they are rather pernicious in that they leave her acted upon or done to in stereotyped and suffocating ways. Her outlet, presented whimsically in *The Edible Woman*, is Duncan whose graduate work removes him, perhaps, from the commercial world that spawns the sex roles that Seymour Surveys tries to codify and enshrine so that potential advertisers need only tap into the models to market their products. Although Duncan is not developed fully as a realistic alternative to the miasma which surrounds Marian, his bohemian style is meant as some kind of antidote to the monolithic "real world."

Whereas *The Edible Woman* has an expansive, jocular character, *Surfacing* has a more terse, laconic tone more in keeping with Atwood's understated poetry. Whereas *The Edible Woman*, *Lady Oracle*, *Life Before Man*, and *Bodily Harm* are prolix, containing the reams of data that prompted Ian Watt to cite verisimilitude as a staple of the novel, *Surfacing* is more elliptical. As a consequence it reads more powerfully than Atwood's other novels, conveying the tortured elements of victimization more poignantly. It alone engages incisively the question of language's role in the enslavement and liberation of self and, by extension, of country.

In "Progressive Insanities of a Pioneer" Atwood writes:

Things
refused to name themselves; refused
to let him name them.[19]

This refusal to be named is central to the rejection of victimization that Atwood's heroines attempt. To be named is to be pigeon-holed, to be categorized and slotted. There is on the part of the protagonist of *Surfacing*, especially, a desire to be reconstituted free of the names imposed upon her because of her role as woman and as colonized Canadian. Gass and Coover can be invoked here as allies in this instance in that Atwood too recognizes that a language straitjackets a people; the yoke to be overthrown is a lexical as well as a cultural one. Atwood, though, would in a political context allow a Canadian language to be substituted for an American one. Atwood has said, "All you can do is opt for the society that seems most humane. People don't seem to function well in very large groups, and that's why I prefer Canada to the States. It's more intimate, and people can still involve themselves in the political process."[20]

Such a sanguine view is not readily apparent in *Surfacing*. The radical stripping of the accretions of civilization, including language, before the naked self emerges, mitigates somewhat the approachable, political note struck in the remark just quoted. Although Atwood does not engage the conventions of fiction as if they were politically loaded; although she does not write her novels with the distrust of the communal language, which Kroetsch maintains is surrendered to unduly, she does force her characters to divest themselves of words as they divest themselves of flesh — in order to discover what is intrinsically, essentially theirs.

The beginning of *Surfacing* is as loaded as that of *The Edible Woman*, in which eating breakfast initiates the food motif presented in the title and the epigraph: "I can't believe I'm on this road again, twisting along past the lake where the white birches are dying, the disease is spreading up from the south, and I notice they now have sea-planes for hire."[21] The disease here is explicitly American, a technological malaise which affects not only the Canadian land but also the narrator. Rather than Marian McAlpine's langourous confrontation with a predator, in *Surfacing* there is an immediate acknowledgement of the enemy and the condition. More aggressive and combative than Marian, the narrator of *Surfacing* asserts at the end of the novel, at the end of her search for that which is essential to her, "This above all, to refuse to be a victim" (*Surfacing*, p. 191). *Surfacing* chronicles her attempt to rid her self of a language and a culture that have victimized and potentially can victimize her. The husked and literal layers of contemporary consciousness are confronted as a deleterious entity in herself and in others. Occasionally, romantically, she thinks of her absent father as having escaped such a consciousness.

Although the mythopoeic elements of the novel are perhaps

overstressed in the above quotation, the heroine's quest is certainly a relentless and radical one. She begins fully formed, caustic, and wise. Jaded in her relationship with her lover, Joe, scarred by an abortion and the disappearance of her father, soured by the inroads made by Americans who are metonymic of modernity, the narrator is primed to dispense with the staples and paraphernalia of her life. Joe is initially linked with the invaders, described on first sight as follows: "From the side he's like the buffalo on the U.S. nickel, shaggy and blunt-snouted, with small clenched eyes and the defiant but insane look of a species once dominant, now threatened with extinction" (*Surfacing*, p. 8). He and the more superficial David are crueler manifestations of the sexist Peter. They use movie cameras to capture and imprison their truths as Peter used his camera for photography. They also talk about baseball, are served by their women, act sexually as predators, and occasionally, when rebuffed, throw tantrums or sulk.

For all their nastiness and shallowness, the men are regarded as less heinous victimizers than Americans.

> [Americans] spread themselves like a virus, they get into the brain and take over the cells and the cells change from inside and the ones that have the disease can't tell the difference. Like the late show sci-fi movies, creatures from outer space, body snatchers injecting themselves into you dispossessing your brain, their eyes blank eggshells behind the dark glasses. If you look like them and talk like them and think like them then you are them,...you speak their language, a language is everything you do. (*Surfacing*, p. 129)

The narrator's hyperbole and shrillness, like Marian's metaphorical assessment of Peter, are directed more at a sensibility, a state of mind, than at a country. The America in *Surfacing*, which is reacted to with the vitriol of a Coover, stands for a contemporary mode of living which disgusts the narrator. Not a disinterested assessor — her abortion and the impending confirmation of her father's drowning spawn a great many images of death — she contracts an insanity which has the same purgative effect as Marian's. For a time she escapes America's inroads and its attendant language. That language, which "is everything you do," is seen to be a lie. Indeed, the narrator's escape from civilization and its language begins in a domestic setting with Joe asking her if she loves him. "It's love, the ritual word, he wants to know again; but I can't give redemption, even as a lie. We both wait for my answer. The wind moves, rustling of tree lungs, water lapping all around us" (*Surfacing*, p. 162). Refusing to speak the clichéd language of sentiment, she proceeds to abandon all but guttural forms of discourse. Dumping the cannisters of film that contain Joe's and David's cinematic efforts, she makes her escape. Later she unburdens herself of other accoutrements of her social world: among them the portfolio of drawings for *Quebec Folk Tales* that she had been commissioned to illustrate and her wedding-band. She begins to live as an elemental and atavistic person, refusing to avail herself of what she calls their definition of sanity: "[t]o have someone to speak to and words that can be understood" (*Surfacing*, p. 190).

Again, here, language becomes the semiotics of entrapment, an appurtenance of the victimizers. Her notion of her essential self in opposition to an accommodatingly normal self becomes the following:

> That is the real danger now, the hospital or the zoo, where we are put, species and individual, when we can no longer cope. They would never believe it's only a natural woman, state of nature, they think of that as a tanned body on a beach with washed hair waving like scarves; not this, face dirt-caked and streaked, skin grimed and scabby, hair like a frayed bathmat stuck with leaves and twigs. A new kind of centrefold. (*Surfacing*, p. 190)

Madness and atavism, though, are not to remain the narrator's locus. They are a prelude to something which is, at the end of *Surfacing*, only potential. "The word games, the winning and losing games are finished; at the moment there are no others but they will have to be invented, withdrawing is no longer possible and the alternative is death" (*Surfacing*, p. 191). With that assertive credo the narrator espouses an as yet uncreated self that is other than American, as well as other than patriarchal. The new language attendant upon the new self is promised as well. The positiveness of her assertion leaves no doubt that, having gone through the purgative and refining process, she will return substantially altered to civilization with Joe who has returned to the wilderness for her one final time.

The upbeat but unspecified ending of *Surfacing* mirrors that of *The Edible Woman*: it also reflects the sternly optimistic, visionary endings of some of Adrienne Rich's work. That incisive poet of woman's roles in a patriarchal society writes, in the final section of "Snapshots of a Daughter-in-Law":

but her cargo
no promise then:
delivered
palpable
ours[22]

After a series of snapshots in which women are portrayed as despoiled and victimized, that final snapshot, a proleptic one, demarcates future roles in an other than patriarchal society. If Coover's "Imagination rules the world, shithead" can be inserted here, it is not so that one fiction can be seen to be replaced by another, but rather that a firmer, truer reality on personal and cultural levels can replace the Americanization that taints all behaviour (especially linguistic and sexual) in *Surfacing*. Of the dead and mutilated heron which recurs occasionally and poignantly in the novel, the narrator asks, "I wondered what part of them the heron was, that they needed so much to kill it" (*Surfacing*, p. 119). The narrator's assessment of the milieu from which she has retreated is that it permeates and aggravates everything.

The target in *Surfacing* is shaped in as clearly and as caricatured a manner as the target in *The Edible Woman*. Nonetheless, the power of *Surfacing*, spare and metaphorical as it is, is considerable. *Lady Oracle* appears on first glance to be a reversion to a simpler mode, the more flip and arch manner of *The Edible Woman*, in its engagement with a theme inherent in all of Atwood's work: the search for a coherent, solid self. Joan Delacourt alias Joan Foster alias Louise K. Delacourt sheds pounds, changes hair colour, and disguises herself at various times in order to reconstitute herself. In addition, she moves to various locales and takes up with various men, maritally and otherwise, in pursuit of a similar end. What gives *Lady Oracle* its added complexity is its protracted concern with the role language plays in sustaining fictions and disguises of diverse kinds. Whereas *Surfacing* is a skeletal study of language in which language and silence reflect civilization and atavism respectively, *Lady Oracle* parades pulp literature of various kinds before the reader. There is a Polish Count who writes nurse novels; Joan, herself, in one phase writes Gothic novels; in another she becomes a celebrity as a result of *Lady Oracle*, a collection of "shlock" poetry which results from her flirtation with automatic writing.

The interplay of writing styles that the characters display and also the ironic juxtaposition of Joan's *Lady Oracle* and Atwood's novel of the same name have led to the following critical assessment:

In this novel Atwood has gathered up the concerns of her earlier novels and has written a satire of the first order, in which social convention is embodied in language. The artist, that prime trickster, survives every device she invents to undermine language, her own credibility, her life and the goodwill of her audience, and she is there at the end with an ingratiating bunch of wilting flowers in her hand. This "portrait" of the artist, *Lady Oracle*, is an hilarious and devastating examination of the motive and craft of fiction. That fiction survives the assault, is the testimony of the book. (Sullivan, p. 49)

If the metafictive notion of the primacy of fiction is somewhat overstressed, the above quotation does encapsulate Atwood's concern in *Lady Oracle* with the stylized languages which in *Surfacing* are the duplicit exports of America. There is also a playful swipe in the novel at the appetites for facile, stereotypic fiction upon which the Polish Count, Louise K. Delacourt, and their publishers capitalize.

Lady Oracle breezily introduces the reader to the narrator's assiduous labours in making herself over. Unlike the angry, tortured narrator of *Surfacing*, she planned her death carefully, faking a drowning that leaves her free to undergo the prototypical renewal so dear to Atwood's heroines. She begins that transformation in Terremoto, Italy, which she had previously visited with her husband. This precipitates the reminiscences and evaluation of her past life which provide the bulk of the novel. One early, trivial scene demonstrates the flaccid response to language which allows its exploitation by advertisers and other purveyors of the language of mass communication. Joan, spying in her drawer the underwear with Sunday / Dimanche embroidered on it, remembers, "*For lovers only*, the ad said, so I bought it to go with my lover. I was a sucker for ads, especially those that promised happiness."[23] Her reminiscences take her further into childhood when she was grossly overweight as well as committed to all the pulp media that Nabokov parodies so well in *Lolita*. "She reads the Brownie handbook to learn how to please her mother and Nancy Drew mysteries to discover how to have a relationship with her elusive father. She studied fashion magazines, movie magazines, *True Confessions*, *True Love* comics" (Sullivan, p. 47). Juxtaposed to those manuscripts that Joan works on in the novel's present is her life itself which melodramatically strains both to catch and to deflate ironically the terror of the romances she writes.

Overall, Atwood's fiction is somewhat anomalous. Its obsession is with character formation and the difficulty of maintaining ontological security. The way languages and imperialist cultures intrude on that security is of related concern. *Bodily Harm* and *Life Before Man*, Atwood's two most recent novels, are trendier, contemporary in a pejorative sense, engaging Caribbean insurrections in the former and a *critique de la vie quotidienne* in the latter. In *Bodily Harm* one of the novel's politicians often chides Rennie for being one of "the sweet Canadians.... They are famous for their goodwill" (*BH*, p. 29). There are also jibes at the role Canadian banks have played in the political arenas of the Caribbean: "There are familiar signs: The Bank of Nova Scotia, The Canadian Imperial Bank of Commerce. The bank buildings are new, the buildings surrounding them are old" (*BH*, p. 69). However, *Bodily Harm* is more potboiler than penetrating look at colonialism or even character; *Life Before Man* is a particularly lifeless and diffuse contribution to the Atwood canon. Given Atwood's acute sense of the implications of language, including the language of fiction, it is surprising that she has been so quick to rule out the political and metaphysical implications of technique in fiction. While the tautness of *Surfacing* sets it slightly apart from the other novels, Atwood's fiction, as opposed to her poetry, reads in a somewhat glib and facile manner. Occasionally engrossing plots outrun any sense of carefully crafted fictions, though the imagistic touch seminal to her poetry has not been completely abandoned in her novels.

In a slim volume on the work of Robertson Davies published in 1972, Elspeth Buitenhuis acknowledges the importance Davies' voice and attitudes play in his novels. She quotes an approving remark of Davies about Robert Smith Surtees, a minor Victorian novelist: "'He is in the thick of his book because he knows very well that he is the best thing it has to offer, and that his knowledge and insight are the marrow of it.'"[24] In the Salterton and Deptford trilogies and the recently published *The Rebel Angels* there is perhaps less of the peevish Davies one finds in an article such as the one he wrote for *The Globe and Mail* denouncing the decade, the seventies, which had just passed (not regretfully according to Davies who rued its unsettling, disruptive character). There is nonetheless in the novels a good deal of discourse, of the pedagogical disquisition. The direct dissemination of ideas through Liesl and Ramsay, Blazon and Parlabane, Eisengrim and Dr. Von Haller comes very thinly disguised from the patrician Davies.

This is not to say that a stuffy, elitist culture preserving itself and its embattled conservatism from a democratic or anarchic rabble is the focus of Davies' novels. Indeed, in an interview with Donald Cameron, Davies mentions that the reception of *A Mixture of Frailties* was mixed largely because those who had liked the first two Salterton novels disliked the last one: "it suggested that I and they had not agreed upon the kind of little provincial city which they could be cozy about...."[25] Also, there are attempts to undermine outmoded ways of talking and living, especially in a Canadian country. A character in *Leaven of Malice* is brusquely told to stop talking as if he were in a novel by Walter Scott. More significantly, the subject of the Salterton novels when they move beyond the tradition of English domestic comedy (an assessment, incidentally, which Davies is at pains to denounce in his interview with Cameron)[26] is Canadian culture and its variegated relationship with England and Europe.

The novels do not simply contain, as Buitenhuis contends they do, an elevation of old-world culture and denigration of Canadian culture. For Davies, though, there is much to deride in the deficiencies of the latter. There is the comical staging of a Shakespearian play in *Tempest-Tost*, the humour emanating from the disjunction between indigenous culture and imported play. There are also the unflattering remarks about a barren culture and its religious rigidity that find their avatar in *Fifth Business:* "One of the things...[our village] conspicuously lacked was an aesthetic sense; we were all too much the descendants of hard-bitten pioneers to wish for or encourage any such thing, and we gave hard names to qualities that, in a more sophisticated society, might have had value";[27] "That horrid village and your hateful Scots family made you a moral monster" (*FB*, p. 217). In addition, Monica Gall in *A Mixture of Frailties* must go to England and Europe to hone her voice and shed her provincialism. The Bridgetower educational project, a condition of the will of Solly Bridgetower's mother, dictates the maintenance abroad of a young woman who might "bring back to Canada some of the intangible treasures of European tradition."[28] When Monica is chosen by the local committee, it decides to elicit the opinion of a touring English conductor, "one of the greatest conductors in the world who was also — this weighed heavily — a British knight!"[29]

Regardless of whether some of the above examples are related ironically, there is the sense in the Deptford trilogy, especially, that Liesl's castle and other such trappings of the old world contain far more potential for the living of a rich, exotic life than does the more mundane Canadian milieu. There is, for instance, in *Leaven of Malice* a witty deflation of the Canadian search for literary roots. Solly, the academic neophyte, is given some career advice by the head of the English department, Dr. Darcy Sengreen: "if I were a young fellow in your position, I wouldn't hesitate for an instant. I'd jump right into Amcan."[30] Sengreen then gives Solly copies of the lugubrious works of Charles Heavysege. Solly drolly imagines himself as "the big man in the Heavysege field," having written one of the very biggest things in Canadian literary studies. He then asks himself more mournfully and despairingly:

> Why do countries have to have literatures? Why does a country like Canada, so late upon the international scene, feel that it must rapidly acquire the trappings of older countries — music of its own, pictures of its own, books of its own — and why does it fuss and stew, and storm the heavens with its outcries when it does not have them? (LM, p. 173)

Davies' answer to these questions that Solly formulates is dualistic. To strain to resurrect fusty tomes with such lines given to *Saul*'s Saul as, "If Prompted, follow me, and be the ball / Tiny at first, that shall, like one of snow, / Gather in rolling" (*LM*, p. 188), is for Davies as well as Solly to redistribute howlers, the yoking of Canadian and Biblical modes producing a rather unsalutary hybrid. Inferior literature remains for Davies inferior literature. Although one can only guess at his vision of a genuine, Canadian literature from his novels, his non-fictional pieces make clear that it will slowly be built out of genuine literature that happens to be Canadian, rather than from such works as Heavysege's or *The Plain That Broke the Plow*, the work-in-progress of Henry Rumball, one of *The Bellman*'s reporters. Rumball's imminent masterpiece was according to him "an epic, there could be no doubt about that. It seemed to become more epic every day. It swept on and on, including more and more aspects of life in the great Canadian West, until he was thoroughly astonished by it" (*LM*, p. 175).

Such unnatural efforts to produce a tradition are to Davies clearly contemptible. His patrician dimensions not only move him to repugnance at such an ersatz tradition, but they also cause him to reject the British tradition when represented by the feckless Bevill Higgin of *Leaven of Malice*. Although Solly is the speaker here and not Davies, himself, the disreputable part Higgin plays in the novel leaves no doubt that Higgin's style is meant to be distasteful to the reader as well as to Solly.

Our British heritage; what a lot was said about it in Canada, one way and another, and it always meant people like Chaucer and Spenser; it never seemed to mean people like Bevill Higgin who were, after all, more frequent ambassadors from the Old Country....But to find the little pipsqueak in the house, mooing Tennyson to all those old trouts in the drawing-room! (*LM*, p. 169)

Clearly, Solly's discomfort extends beyond his personal response. It recalls very clearly the false importation of culture that the Duke and the Dauphin of Mark Twain's *Adventures of Huckleberry Finn* use to dupe the gullible unsophisticated folk of rural America. Twain's purpose is to reveal the inappropriateness of that foreign culture to a truly American sensibility. Davies has a different perspective on the matter. In his interview with Donald Cameron he tells of going to see a production of Anton Chekhov's *The Cherry Orchard* in Cobourg, Ontario, and being surprised at the evening dress of many of the other patrons. He calls their dress and their reception of the play "a sort of delayed cultural tradition." He goes on to say, "About the period that I was working on the Salterton novels, just after the 1945 war, there were still people living in places like Salterton whose tradition was directly Edwardian, and who saw nothing wrong with that."[31] Davies sees nothing wrong with that — except when it is imported by the likes of Higgin who, it can be presumed, is a shabby, false purveyor of the British heritage. Higgin disgusts Davies not because he quotes Tennyson — which was Twain's more radical stance — but because he quotes him in the way that he does. Charitably, one could say he is reprehensible to the author because he does not genuinely like or study Tennyson; rather, he is trying to impress his audience. Uncharitably, one could say that he is reprehensible to the author because he does not quote Tennyson as a distinguished professor at Massey College or, in the context of *The Rebel Angels*, at the "Guest Night" of the College of St. John and the Holy Ghost. Although the former interpretation makes more sense in the context of *Leaven of Malice*, the latter appeals to this reader at any rate after reading the purportedly enlightened, convivial chatter in which the "Guest Night" guests indulge. Whereas for Twain, the introduction of British tradition into North America is inappropriate, for Davies it can be a salutary thing. This may not be so, however, for the *hoi polloi* or even for Solly's undergraduates whose papers appropriated that tradition poorly. As he grades papers Solly muses, "to begin thinking about Chaucer, or even common sense, was fatal" (*LM*, p. 169).

The clash in Davies' novels, then, is not strictly between indigenous and imported modes of living; it is between enriched and inferior ones. Nonetheless, for the most part the modes Davies advocates savouring are those with an exalted, but genuine, heritage. Rural Canada is the object of Davies' wrath only when it accommodates ersatz values; Davies is sometimes generous to the communities he depicts. This is especially the case in the Salterton novels which reveal little of contemporary society and mores, only as befits the habits of provincial Ontario at the time. These novels show the ironies, contradictions, hypocrisies, limitations, and beneficences of anachronistic, small-town Ontario. The plots are simple and light-hearted, many of the characters, especially the evil ones, such as Higgin, caricatured and modest in their evil-doing. The Deptford novels range much more widely over terrain that is intellectually and physically exotic. As is well known, *Fifth Business*, *The Manticore*, and *World of Wonders* all tell the story of the consequences of that childhood event in which Dunstan Ramsay ducks a snowball intended for him by Boy Staunton. That snowball contains a stone; moreover, it hits a pregnant Mary Dempster causing her to give birth to her son, Paul, prematurely. Dunstan, David Staunton, Boy's son, and Paul who becomes Magnus Eisengrim, a world famous conjurer and illusionist, tell their stories in each of the three novels remembering and relating the events with only occasional interruptions or comments that were precipitated by the snowball throwing incident.

This technique allows the teller to be assured of his tale and in control. Again, while it is dangerous to associate Davies too closely with Dunstan Ramsay, there are those generalizations about mankind's lot and the ways of the world that give the novels, for all the fantastical events such as Paul's transformation into Magnus and the adventurous life he led after his escape from Deptford, a static, didactic quality: for instance, of Diana Marfleet with whom Dunstan becomes intimate while recuperating from his grievous war wounds and who falls in love with him, Dunstan related that she makes "one of those feminine leaps in logic that leave men breathless" (*FB*, p. 91). Regarding Sam West, a friend of Dunstan's father, he tells of that man's ability to find contradictions in the Bible; one of Dunstan's summations is, "I have known many atheists since Sam, and they all fall down on metaphor" (*FB*, p. 55).

This last quotation provides a clue to one of the major values inculcated in *Fifth Business*, specifically, and the trilogy, generally. When Liesl utters, "Now tell me how you are going to get the infant Magnus

Eisengrim out of that dreadful Canada and into a country where big spiritual adventures are possible?" (*FB*, p. 218) she defines the quest for Ramsay and the other main characters of the trilogy as well. Ramsay's big spiritual adventures are related in *Fifth Business* as a response, he tells us, to the condescending farewell to him in the *College Chronicle*, on the occasion of his retirement. He feels that the farewell inadequately encapsulates his life. A passionate hagiographer Ramsay accorded Mrs. Dempster the status of sainthood (crediting her with saving his brother from death), this despite the discovery of her fornicating with a tramp in a pit near Deptford.

Davies' sense of the richness of life is given expression by and large by his iconoclasts, for instance, devout clergymen such as Padre Blazon of *Fifth Business* and Parlabane of *The Rebel Angels*; these men are passionate believers who are also worldly, who savour food and/or sex inordinately, and whose carnal dimensions are as fully developed as their cerebral and spiritual ones. Soon after Ramsay sees Padre Blazon for the last time and is told that he has led the heroic life, Ramsay finally fulfills the quest that nominally forms the framework of *Fifth Business*. During an attack in World War I which nearly killed him and left him claudicant, he had had a vision of a religious icon, a Madonna, which he had linked to Mary Dempster.

> [Padre Blazon] was much in my mind as I tasted the pleasures of Salzburg, and particularly so after my first visit to the special display called *Schöne Madonnen*, in the exhibition rooms in the Cathedral. For here, at last, and after having abandoned hope and forgotten my search, I found the little Madonna I had seen during my bad night at Passchendaele. (*FB*, pp. 250-51)

Davies' vision, part humanistic, part mystical, is embodied primarily in Ramsay who is the eponymous hero of the novel, an essential yet not dominating "Fifth Business" of the definition that prefaces the novel. Ramsay's secondary role does not minimize his achievements. Born to a provincial Ontario family, maimed in the war, he gains what Buitenhuis calls a religious view of the world. In contrast to Boy Staunton who is materialistic and limited, Ramsay opens himself to chance and allows himself to experience the different pleasures and insights accorded by Liesl, Magnus, and Padre Blazon. Buitenhuis aptly quotes the world view to which Ramsay does not subscribe:

121

Where shall wisdom be found, and where is the place of understanding? Not among Boy Staunton's ca-pittle-ists, nor among the penniless scheme-spinners in the school Common Room, nor yet at the Social Communist meetings in the city, which were sometimes broken up by the police. I seemed to be the only person I knew without a plan that would put the world on its feet and wipe the tear from every eye. (*FB*, pp. 167-68)

Ramsay's world of wonders is an apolitical, magical realm inhabited by conjurers such as Eisengrim, and those such as Blazon who are both passionately spiritual and passionately physical — people in short with tutored as opposed to gross appetites, with a mixture of learning, nobility, and carnality.

Despite the avowal of Dunstan that he is anti-utopian and "without a plan that would put the world on its feet," the final two novels of the Deptford trilogy contain a good deal of sermonizing and, especially in the case of *The Manticore*, far too little of the magical. This is so in *The Manticore* despite David Staunton's own search for vitality and the heroic life. David's story is told by him retrospectively to Doctor Johanna Von Haller, a Zurich disciple of Jung to whom he has gone for psychotherapy. By retelling from his own perspective the same story by and large that Ramsay relates in *Fifth Business*, he learns to overcome his family legacy, his own ratiocinative bias, and his country's legacy: "in Canada we geld everything if we can...."[32] David's sense of the world, even as he matures, owes a great deal to Ramsay's and to Davies' conservative ideology:

> when I see girls who have not yet attained their full growth storming the legislatures for abortion on demand, and adolescents pressing their right to freedom to have intercourse whenever and however they please, and read books advising women that anal intercourse is a jolly lark (provided both partners are "squeaky clean"), I wonder.... (*M*, pp. 167-68)

Strongly evoking Davies' aforementioned cranky diatribe in *The Globe and Mail*, these spleenful remarks of David's appear to be gratuitous, insofar as the thrust of his psychotherapy is to move him towards becoming a more balanced thinking-feeling being. Also, David is digressing here in the story of his love for Judy, a childhood sweetheart. It is true that at the behest of his father David has hired someone to ferret out the Staunton line and is quite delighted to discover he descends from a feisty woman who produces a bastard son. Again, though, Davies' novels alternate between an energy and appetite that are joyful and enriching for some and those characteristics that, when translated into demotic culture, are baneful for civilization.

His elitist remarks notwithstanding, David exorcises the demons of his past in a particularly unsuspenseful way, then encounters Liesl, Magnus, and Dunstan, going with them to her castle which becomes a kind of finishing school. He is scolded by Liesl for not being a Nietzschean *Übermensch*:

> just because you are not a roaring egotist, you needn't fall for the fashionable modern twaddle of the anti-hero and the mini-soul. That is what we might call the Shadow of democracy; it makes it so laudable, so cosy and right and easy to be a spiritual runt and lean on all the other runts for support and applause in a splendid apotheosis of runtdom. (*M*, p.268)

With these invigorating words Liesl takes David on a risky outing, spelunking, to see if he can find the heroic essence of himself that presumably will remove him even further from the company of those women who demand abortions, copulate promiscuously, and read books advocating sodomy. That his fear in the cave causes him to shit his drawers (speaking in the plain style Dunstan Ramsay champions) does not preclude his finding the heroic dimension. Ramsay's benediction at the end of the novel confirms David's success, his recognition that "if we are really wise, we will make a working arrangement with the bear that lives with us, because otherwise we shall starve or perhaps be eaten by the bear" (*M*, p.279). Thus restored and healed David ends his tale with the declaration that he will no longer shirk his responsibilities.

World of Wonders is Magnus Eisengrim's tale, the story told by him of his life as Paul Dempster and as the internationally renowned Eisengrim. There is nothing here to recall Atwood's characters whose shifts of identity are desperate attempts to discover the reality beneath appearances. Eisengrim's various transformations are, rather, circumstantial. First, he is taken on by Willard as his "bum boy" and operator of Abdullah, the "mechanical" card-sharp that takes the rubes who turn up at the carnivals set up by Willard's employers. In England his resemblance to Sir John Tresize and his acrobatic abilities land him a job as Sir John's double and stuntman. Then he is taken up by Liesl's grandfather as a toy repairer; afterwards he and Liesl develop the conjuring act which made him world famous and which caused him to be recruited to play Houdini. It is during and after the filming of "Un Hommage à Robert-Houdin" that Eisengrim tells his story.

Among others, Liesl augments Eisengrim's narrative with the commentary that ties into Ramsay's tale and his absorption with saints and mythology. She credits Eisengrim with having what Spengler called the "Magian World View," a view shared it is clear by the rest of Liesl's coterie as well.

> It was a sense of the unfathomable wonder of the invisible world that existed side by side with a hard recognition of the roughness and cruelty and day-to-day demands of the tangible world. It was a readiness to see demons where nowadays we see neuroses, and to see the hand of a guardian angel in what we are apt to shrug off ungratefully as a stroke of luck. It was religion, but a religion with a thousand gods, none of them all-powerful and most of them ambiguous in their attitude toward man. It was poetry and wonder which might reveal themselves in the dunghill, and it was an understanding of the dunghill that lurks in poetry and wonder.[33]

This passage is quoted at such length because it contains the quintessential thrust of the Deptford trilogy. Modernity, rationalism, popularism, and, not irrelevantly, a Canada of religious orthodoxy and narrowness — all are deleterious to the "Magian World View." The last word of the trilogy, directed at Ramsay but meant approvingly for Liesl and Eisengrim as well, is egoist. Egoism proves to be a strong force in those characters Davies draws positively. It provides the impetus to live in a way that is unconventional yet genteel, religious yet worldly.

The Rebel Angels continues to celebrate such notions. The gypsy strains of Maria Theotoky, the non-pedantic scholarly ways of Clement Hollier, the wonder and poetry of Parlabane's dunghill — these are the touted heart of that novel. That it is set in Canada is meant to show presumably that the world of wonders can be rooted there as elsewhere. The fusty conversations of the scholars on their interminable Guest Nights, though, do not make a convincing case for exoticism. One of the scholars says wittily, "Academicism runs in the blood like syphilis."[34] If so, Nietzsche was far wiser than those contemporary scholars in, so the probably apocryphal story goes, purposefully contracting syphilis — the real thing, not the weaker academic strain.

Whereas Atwood's heroines fight to regain, preserve, or discover their shaky selves, and anorexia becomes a prominent metaphor in that regard, Davies' heroes are well fed — "A good meal should be a performance; the Edwardians understood that"[35] — unsure only of the ontological status of others less magian than they are. Such bulking up, nonetheless, does nothing to nourish those impoverished Canadians whom Eisengrim remembers in his carnival and theatrical tours of Canada as having only refracted English sustenance, "happy just to be listening to English voices repeating noble sentiments."[36] Colonial fare is very much at the heart of Davies' enterprise; moreover, it is by no means to be disgorged the way many Canadian nationalists would react to American servings. Very clearly Davies' characters and he, himself, are nourished by dollops of literate and genteel culture, regardless of its origin, but primarily of the variety of "the great tradition."

David Staunton often extols Ramsay's espousal of the plain style. Insofar as the form of Davies' fiction is concerned, that clearly if unheedingly means the British style—the traditional novel with narrative and social underpinnings. In other words, the tradition has been subsumed into the supposedly neutral, natural, plain style. The experiments, what Davies would probably regard as aberrations, signify and they do so the way protest groups and dissidents do to Davies, in a way which is anathema to him. In an insightful remark, cited in a *New York Review of Books* essay by Alexander Cockburn, Frank MacShane differentiates between English and American styles:

> "[American style] is a fluid language, like Shakespearian English, and easily takes in new words, new meanings for old words.... Its overtones and undertones are not stylized into a social conventional kind of subtlety which is in effect a class language. It is more alive to clichés.... English, being on the defensive, is static and cannot contribute anything but a sort of waspish criticism of forms and manners...."[37]

MacShane goes on to call good English a class language and the English writer a gentleman first and a writer second.

It seems to me that Davies' work, as well as much of the rest of Canadian fiction, except the kind written by Kroetsch and the other writers examined in the preceding chapter, is clearly British stylistically. It accepts a norm for form (and for manners, too) that never enters the foreground of the fiction. In Atwood's case the refusal to concern herself with the form of fiction is a conscious, political choice — questions of identity are of paramount concern and negate what she might regard as effete formal considerations. Davies, for all his sympathy with the rebel angels who people his novels, is clearly a gentleman first and a writer second, the deployment of the plain style being for him a much more unconscious act than it is for Atwood. Regardless, both writers' focus and fiction are clearly ontological rather than epistemological, to return to Bowering's formulation for the difference between the modern and the postmodern or contemporary. That makes their fiction more British than American and differentiates them more sharply from Coover and Gass than from Malcolm Bradbury and Iris Murdoch and even Ian MacEwan. To regard the staples of fiction as loaded with signification is something Atwood does not wish and Davies does not think to do. That the novel has a heritage is enough, certainly for Davies. Frederick Bowers' question, cited in Chapter One, was "Why is it that of the many able craftsmen writing in Britain so few have experimented with form...?" That same question asked of Canada can be answered by demonstrating Canada's affinities, insofar as fiction is concerned, with tepid British variations as well as its writers' desires to nourish the Canadian identity.

Conclusion

A RECENT BRIEF REVIEW of Margaret Atwood's *Dancing Girls and Other Stories* in *The Review of Contemporary Fiction* concludes with the following dismissal: "Why would anyone want to read these stories? Why would anyone want to write them?"[1] To Canadians reared on William French's encomia in *The Globe and Mail* or other such effusive statements by the doyens of Canadian letters, such an appraisal is shocking, even incomprehensible; it is akin to a call for the banishment of Shakespeare from the literary firmament. The comparison is not inapposite. For a conservative or Arnoldian critic, a rebuke to a "great" writer or to the "tradition," challenges his *raison d'être* which he clearly believes to be one of conservation. The Canadian critic shares that ideology. He sees his role as the shaping, grooming, and readying for distribution and assimilation of a national literature. In a sense his role is hagiographical as is the Arnoldian role.

Literary criticism can be thought of in another way, one crystallized recently by Terry Eagleton in *Literary Theory: An Introduction* and by Edward Said in *The World, The Text and The Critic*. Both, influenced enormously by Foucault, tout the activity rather than the object, the trophy. Both display an irreverence to the inviolable, ahistorical work of art. Said writes: "the moment anything acquires the status of a cultural idol...it ceases to be interesting."[2] The classics, the great writer and his analysable oeuvre, indeed, "literature" as some certifiable and integral entity are, so Eagleton and Said argue, the products of political acts of inclusion and exclusion rather than inherently proper and natural categories.

Clearly, throughout the foregoing chapters my sympathy has been for this latter stance. Similarly, regarding the two antithetical modes of writing fiction that predominate in English Canada and the United States, ontological and modern in the first case, epistemological and postmodern in the second, my predilection has again been for the latter. While it is perhaps understandable that the fiction of Atwood and Robertson Davies has been over-praised, it is not fully forgivable. Literature dragooned into the service of the state has its vitality undermined. Being on Her Majesty's service or facsimile thereof adulterates, if not devalues, the literary activity.

That nationalism is an unmitigated good is surely a notion that should have currency on a parliamentary or legislative rather than on a literary level (if it has any standing at all). Of course it makes sense that when a country feels itself threatened culturally by another it will embark on a project to solidify its identity; however, whether that project demands the enthusiastic endorsement of its novelists is a much more tenuous issue. Roch Carrier's warning about the displacement of Québécois artists in the Parti Québécois' assumption of power is an apt one. While one does not want the kind of situation contemporary American novelists have found themselves in, namely a hostile and combative relationship with the country's image and activities — a situation that is replicated in other countries with consequences far more severe and threatening — one should also be leery of the seemingly more sublime mandate of helping to articulate where "here" is. "Here," surely, when it is defined in geo-political terms is a somewhat specious place, the conventions demarcating it as arbitrary and relative as those which give realistic fiction its popularity. If team uniforms and game rules are the semiotics of sport, then the conventions and mannerisms of which "here" is often so proudly comprised are the semiotics of nationalism. Although these may be necessary pragmatically, they need not be Mount Pisgah to which the writer conducts his reader.

The writer in the United States demands no such following, articulates no such goal. He courts exclusion, subverting rather than assenting to political goals. The Canadian writer cultivates a more socially acceptable image. Almost the solid citizen, he often speaks for his country, its aspirations and needs. His acceptance of the trappings of traditional fiction reveals his conservatism.

Literature, though, has an anarchistic dimension that, despite the conventions it acknowledges, allows it to flourish in climes usually inimical to it and that because of its unruliness tends to prevent its assimilation in a nationalization program. Literary criticism, however, has not, except perhaps in the hands of the deconstructionists, had that undermining quality. Rather, its function has been primarily the domestication of art, effected by synthesizing meaning and divulging how technique can shape and assist that meaning. Literary criticism in Canada, especially, has for some time operated with ardour to foster Canadian nationalism. Despite the chiding it received from Frank Davey, among others, it has insularly maintained its direction. Perhaps this is as a result of the more directly political and institutional dimensions of the university as opposed to those minimal forces which dictate to artists in the so-called free world; recently, the pressures for scholars to be Canadian and to teach and study Canadian authors has intensified. Perhaps too, the stolid British strain which has cultivated the classics not to the exclusion but certainly to the relegation of contemporary literature is dominant in the Canadian academic milieu.

Such a stance which had in part been responsible for the rejection of Canadian literary models now works effectively to install those models in the panoply of the tradition, of the classics. While the consequences of this critical framework may not seem to be debilitating, and may in fact appear to be beneficent, they do have deleterious offshoots. Criticism loses its feistiness; it lives sycophantically off Canadian literature, only its "read Canadian" being heard. It also appears to be far more homogeneous than that practised in the United States. It is certainly a long way from the guerrilla warfare notion of literary criticism enunciated by Michel Foucault: "Writing only interests me to the extent that it unites itself to the reality of a combat, functioning as an instrument, a tactic, an illumination. I would like my books to be sorts of scalpels, Molotov cocktails, or minefields...."[3] The Canadian critic does not feel embattled to the extent that he need go underground; rather, he is comfortably ensconced as the arbiter of literary values in Canada. Survival is no longer the issue; rather, isolationism and complacency need to be confronted.

Ironically, the situation of the literary critic in the United States is a more tenuous one. With no role to play in the formation of a national identity, the critic, should he wish to appeal broadly to his countrymen, has to resort to a bromide such as the one articulated by the Rockefeller Foundation sponsored Commission on the Humanities: "This commission believes that the humanities are a social good and that their well-being is in the national interest."[4] Uplift of this kind might sound strange to readers of contemporary American fiction and to proponents of deconstruction. It might, that is, until one realizes that American critics employed by universities subsist on public (governmental or institutional) funds. Thus, despite the ferment that deconstruction has caused in academic circles, it has been appropriated for methodological rather than social forays. The literary critic, peripherally placed in the "real world" of commerce, studies Robert Coover and William Gass to build a career instead of a nation; despite the disproportionately sized edifice, it is a similar enterprise. Nevertheless, some individual critics such as Said, Ihab Hassan, and Richard Ohmann have resisted and even rebuked that venture. Even more mutinously, writers of metafiction confront systems, national and personal, of all kinds. Without as much critical credibility and therefore prominence, a few Canadian writers have been as combative. Their story (history) needs, perhaps, only to be told for the Canadian emphasis to be altered.

Notes

CHAPTER ONE: CATHECTIC AMERICA: ANORECTIC CANADA

[1] Margaret Atwood, "Two-Headed Poem," in her *Two-Headed Poems* (New York: Simon and Schuster, 1978), p. 59.

[2] Kildare Dobbs, "Canada's Regions," in *Profile of a Nation*, ed. Alan Dawe (Toronto: Macmillan, 1969), p. 64.

[3] Dobbs, p. 68.

[4] Joyce Nelson, "Global Pillage: The Economics of Commercial Television," in *Love and Money: The Politics of Culture*, ed. D. Helwig (Ottawa: Oberon, 1980), p. 31.

[5] Stephen Spender, *Love-Hate Relations: A Study of English and American Sensibilities* (New York: Random House, 1974), pp. xvi-xvii. All further references to this work appear in the text.

[6] Jack Hicks, *In the Singer's Temple: Prose Fictions of Barthelme, Gaines, Brautigan, Piercy, Kesey, and Kosinski* (Chapel Hill: Univ. of North Carolina Press, 1981), p. 12. All further references to this work appear in the text.

[7] Alexis de Tocqueville, *Democracy in America*, II (New York: The Colonial, 1899), p. 59.

[8] Frederick Bowers, "An Irrelevant Parochialism," *Granta*, I, No. 3 (1980), 150.

[9] Bill Buford, Introduction, *Granta*, I, No. 3 (1980), 9. All further references to this work appear in the text.

[10] Paul Denham and Mary Jane Edwards, eds., Introduction in *Canadian Literature in the 70's* (Toronto: Holt, Rinehart and Winston, 1980), p. xvii. All further references to this work appear in the text.

[11] Robert Kroetsch, "The Canadian Writer and the American Literary Tradition," *English Quarterly*, 4 (Summer 1971), 46.

[12] Northrop Frye, "Journey without Arrival, A Personal Point of View," *The Globe and Mail*, 6 April 1976, p. 7.

[13] Frye, p. 7.

[14] Robert Coover, "Love Scene," *A Theological Position* (New York: Dutton, 1972), p. 98.

[15] Irving Howe, "The American Voice," *The New York Times Book Review*, 4 July 1976, p. 1.

[16] D. H. Lawrence, *Studies in Classic American Literature* (New York: Viking, 1964), p. 54.

[17] Walt Whitman, "Preface 1855-*Leaves of Grass*," in *Leaves of Grass* (New York: Norton, 1973), p. 711.

[18] John Lahr, "Dreamers of the Day," *Harper's*, Jan. 1981, p. 72.

[19] F. Scott Fitzgerald, *The Great Gatsby* (New York: Scribner's, 1925), p. 118.

[20] Fitzgerald, p. 217.

[21] Brendan Gill, *Lindbergh Alone* (New York: Harcourt, Brace, Jovanovich, 1977), p. 14.

[22] Kurt Vonnegut, *Breakfast of Champions* (New York: Delacorte, 1973), p. 10.

[23] Ihab Hassan, *Paracriticisms: Seven Speculations of the Times* (Urbana: Univ. of Illinois, 1975), p. 176. All further references to this work appear in the text.

[24] Norm Goldstein, *John Wayne: A Tribute* (New York: Holt, Rinehart and Winston, 1979), p. 129.

[25] Jane Kramer, *The Last Cowboy* (New York: Harper and Row, 1977), p. 7.

[26] Robert Pirsig, *Zen and the Art of Motorcycle Maintenance* (New York: Morrow, 1974), pp. 289–90.

[27] John Updike, *Rabbit Redux* (New York: Fawcett Crest, 1971), p. 114.

[28] Allen Ginsberg, "America," in *The Postmoderns: The New American Poetry Revised*, ed. D. Allen and G. Butterick (New York: Grove, 1982), p. 184.

[29] Mas'ud Zavarzadeh, *The Mythopoeic Reality: The Postwar American Non-fiction Novel* (Urbana: Univ. of Illinois, 1976), pp. 22–23.

[30] George Steiner, "The Archives of Eden," *Salmagundi* (Fall 1980–Winter 1981), p. 85.

[31] E. L. Doctorow, "False Documents," *American Review: The Magazine of New Writing*, No. 26 (Nov. 1977), p. 217.

[32] William Gass, *Fiction and the Figures of Life* (New York: Knopf, 1970), p. 5. All further references to this work (*FFL*) appear in the text.

[33] Doctorow, p. 232.

[34] Alain Robbe-Grillet, *For a New Novel*, trans. R. Howard (New York: Grove, 1965), p. 156.

[35] Margaret Atwood, *Survival: A Thematic Guide to Canadian Literature* (Toronto: House of Anansi, 1972), pp. 18–19.

[36] Robert Kroetsch, "Beyond Nationalism: A Prologue," *Mosaic*, 14 (Spring 1981), v. All further references to this work appear in the text.

[37] Thomas Pynchon, *The Crying of Lot 49* (New York: Bantam, 1982), p. 137.

[38] Vladimir Nabokov, *Lolita* (New York: Berkley, 1977), p. 32. All further references to this work appear in the text.

[39] Ross Wetzsteon, "Nabokov as Teacher," *TriQuarterly*, No. 17 (Winter 1970), p. 240. All further references to this work appear in the text.

40 Michel Foucault, *The Order of Things* (New York: Vintage, 1973), p. xxiii.

41 Earle Birney, "Canada: Case History," in *Profile of a Nation*, p. 226.

42 Birney, p. 226.

43 Edgar Z. Friedenberg, *Deference to Authority: The Case of Canada* (New York: Sharpe, 1980), p. 32.

44 Pirsig, p. 326.

45 George Bowering, "Modernism Could Not Last Forever," *Canadian Fiction Magazine*, Nos. 32–33 (1979–1980), p. 5. All further references to this work appear in the text.

46 Frances W. Kaye, "The 49th Parallel and the 98th Meridian: Some Lines for Thought," *Mosaic*, 14 (Spring 1981), 166.

47 Friedenberg, pp. 153, 155.

48 Beverly J. Rasporich, "The Leacock Persona and the Canadian Character," *Mosaic*, 14, 88.

49 Robert Kroetsch, "For Play and Entrance: The Contemporary Canadian Long Poem," *Open Letter*, Fifth Series, No. 4 (1983), 107–08.

50 Frank Davey, "Surviving the Paraphrase," *Canadian Literature*, No. 70 (Autumn 1976), p. 6.

51 Jacques Derrida, *Writing and Difference*, trans. Alan Bass (Chicago: Univ. of Chicago Press, 1978), p. 76. All further references to this work appear in the text.

52 Theo Quayle Dombrowski, "Word and Fact: Laurence and the Problem of Language," *Canadian Literature*, No. 80 (1979), pp. 50–62.

53 In *Canadian Literature*, No. 77.

54 Dennis Lee, *Savage Fields: An Essay in Literature and Cosmology* (Toronto: House of Anansi, 1977), p. 32.

55 Barbara Godard, "My (m)Other, My Self: Strategies for Subversion in Atwood and Hébert," *Essays on Canadian Writing*, No. 26 (1983), pp. 13–45.

56 Barry Cameron and Michael Dixon, "Minus Canadian," *Studies in Canadian Literature*, 2 (Summer 1977), 137.

57 Cameron and Dixon, 138.

58 Cameron and Dixon, 138.

59 W. H. New, *Among Worlds: An Introduction to Modern Commonwealth and South African Fiction* (Erin, Ont.: Porcépic, 1975), p. 101.

60 Robertson Davies, "The Canada of Myth and Reality," in *Canadian Literature in the 70's*, ed. Denham and Edwards, p. 9.

61 Roch Carrier, "The Party Is the Pen," *Books in Canada*, Feb. 1979, p. 14. All further references to this work appear in the text.

62 Davies, p. 12.

63 Charles Molesworth, "Reflections," *Salmagundi*, No. 50–51, 103.

[64] Carole Corbeil, "*Aurora!*," *The Globe and Mail*, 27 Sept. 1980, p. 17.

CHAPTER TWO: AMERICA: GASS AND COOVER

[1] Thomas Pynchon, *The Crying of Lot 49* (New York: Bantam, 1982), p. 2.
[2] Pynchon, p. 58.
[3] Pynchon, p. 128.
[4] Ken Kesey, *One Flew Over the Cuckoo's Nest* (New York: Viking, 1964), p. 38.
[5] Kesey, p. 8.
[6] Donald Barthelme, *Sadness* (New York: Farrar, Straus & Giroux, 1972), p. 12.
[7] Barthelme, p. 13.
[8] Donald Barthelme, "The Great Debate," *The New Yorker*, 3 May 1976, pp. 34–35.
[9] Donald Barthelme, *The Dead Father* (New York: Farrar, Straus & Giroux, 1975), p. 125.
[10] Donald Barthelme, *Snow White* (New York: Atheneum, 1982), p. 44.
[11] Roland Barthes, *Mythologies*, trans. Annette Lavers (New York: Hill and Wang, 1972), p. 140. All further references to this work appear in the text.
[12] A.B. Paulson, "The Minnesota Multiphasic Personality: a diagnostic test in two parts," *TriQuarterly*, No. 29 (Winter 1974), p. 208.
[13] Alan Goldfein, *Heads: A Metafictional History of Western Civilization, 1762–1975* (New York: Morrow, 1973), p. 153.
[14] William Gass, *Fiction and the Figures of Life* (New York: Knopf, 1970), p. 25. All further references to this work (*FFL*) appear in the text.
[15] William Gass, *Omensetter's Luck* (New York: Signet, 1967), p. 162. All further references to this work (*OL*) appear in the text.
[16] Ihab Hassan, "Wars of Desire, Politics of the Word," *Salmagundi*, No. 55, 118.
[17] William Gass, Preface in *In the Heart of the Heart of the Country* (Boston: Godine, 1981), p. xvii. All further references to this preface appear in the text.
[18] Ross Wetzsteon, "Nabokov as Teacher," *TriQuarterly* (Winter 1970).
[19] Gustave Flaubert, *Selected Letters*, trans. Francis Steegmuller, in *The Modern Tradition*, ed. R. Ellman and C. Feidelson (New York: Oxford Univ. Press, 1965), p. 126.
[20] André Gide, *The Counterfeiters*, trans. Dorothy Bussy, in Ellman and Feidelson, p. 127.
[21] Michel Foucault, *The Archaeology of Knowledge and the Discourse on*

Language, trans. A. M. Sheridan Smith (New York: Harper, 1972), p. 48.

[22] William Gass, *In the Heart of the Heart of the Country* (New York: Harper & Row, 1968), p. 169. All further references to this work (*HHC*) appear in the text.

[23] William Gass, *Willie Master's Lonesome Wife* (New York: Knopf, 1971), n. pag.

[24] William Gass, "Representation & the War for Reality," *Salmagundi*, No. 55 (Winter 1982), p. 63.

[25] Barthelme, p. 6.

[26] E. L. Doctorow, "False Documents," p. 232.

[27] W.B. Yeats, "Byzantium," *Poems of W. B. Yeats*, selected by A. Norman Jeffares (London: Macmillan Education, 1962), p. 142.

[28] Mas'ud Zavarzadeh, Rev. of *The Pursuit of Signs*, by Jonathan Culler, *The Journal of Aesthetics and Art Criticism*, Spring 1982, p. 330. All further references to this work appear in the text.

[29] W. B. Yeats, "The Circus Animals' Desertion," p. 181.

[30] John Barth, "The Literature of Exhaustion," *Atlantic Monthly*, Aug. 1967.

[31] John Barth, "The Literature of Replenishment," *Atlantic Monthly*, Jan. 1980.

[32] Robert Coover, "The Last Quixote," *New American Review*, No. 11 (1971), p. 136. All further references to this work appear in the text.

[33] Robert Coover, *Pricksongs and Descants* (New York: E.P. Dutton, 1969), p. 77. All further references to this work (*Pricksongs*) appear in the text.

[34] Robert Coover, *A Theological Position* (New York: Dutton, 1972), p. 97.

[35] Coover, *A Theological Position*, p. 169.

[36] Robert Coover, *The Universal Baseball Assoc., Inc.: J. Henry Waugh, Prop.* (New York: Random House, 1968), p. 221. All further references to this work (*UBA*) appear in the text.

[37] Barbara Foley, "From *U.S.A.* to *Ragtime*: Notes on the Forms of Historical Consciousness in Modern Fiction," *American Literature*, 50, No. 1 (1978), 95.

[38] Georg Lukacs, *The Historical Novel* (London: Merlin, 1962), p. 59.

[39] Lukacs, p. 34.

[40] Mas'ud Zavarzadeh, *The Mythopoeic Reality* (Urbana: Univ. of Illinois Press, 1976), p. 66.

[41] Truman Capote, *In Cold Blood* (New York: Signet, 1965), p. 61.

[42] Norman Mailer, *Miami and the Siege of Chicago* (New York: World Publishing Co., 1968), p. 17.

[43] Robert Coover, *The Public Burning* (New York: Viking, 1977), p. 463. All subsequent references to this work (*PB*) appear in the text.

⁴⁴Robert Towers, "Nixon's Seventh Crisis," *The New York Review of Books*, 29 Sept. 1979, p. 8.

⁴⁵Alain Robbe-Grillet, "Order and Disorder in Film and Fiction," *Critical Inquiry*, 4, No. 1 (1977), 10-11.

⁴⁶Jonathan Culler, *Structuralist Poetics* (Ithaca, N.Y.: Cornell Univ. Press, 1975), pp. 264-65.

⁴⁷Ronald Barthes, *Ronald Barthes*, trans. R. Howard (New York: Hill and Wang, 1977). All subsequent references to this work (*RB*) appear in the text.

⁴⁸James Fenimore Cooper, *The Last of the Mohicans* (New York: Signet, 1962), p. 212.

⁴⁹John Barth, *The Sot-Weed Factor* (New York: Bantam, 1969), p. 805.

CHAPTER THREE: ROBERT KROETSCH: FIGURE OF RAPPROCHEMENT

¹Geoff Hancock, "An Interview with Robert Kroetsch," *Canadian Fiction Magazine*, Nos. 24-25 (1977), 39. All further references to this work appear in the text.

²Robert Kroetsch, "The Canadian Writer and the American Literary Tradition," *English Quarterly*, 4 (Summer 1971), 47.

³Peter Thomas, *Robert Kroetsch*, Studies in Canadian Literature, No. 13 (Vancouver: Douglas & McIntyre, 1980), p. 116. All further references to this work appear in the text.

⁴Geoff Hancock, "An Interview with Leon Rooke," *Canadian Fiction Magazine*, No. 38 (1981), pp. 108-09.

⁵John Barth, *Lost in the Funhouse* (New York: Bantam, 1969), p. 123.

⁶Martin Myers, *The Assignment* (New York: Ballantine, 1971), pp. 326-27. All further references to this work appear in the text.

⁷Ray Smith, "Dinosaur," in *The Narrative Voice*, ed. John Metcalf (Toronto: McGraw-Hill Ryerson, 1969), p. 117.

⁸Smith, p. 206.

⁹Ray Smith, *Cape Breton Is the Thought Control Centre of Canada* (Toronto: House of Anansi, 1969), p. 17.

¹⁰David McFadden, *The Great Canadian Sonnet* (Toronto: Coach House, 1974), p. 104.

¹¹John Riddell, *Criss-Cross* (Toronto: Coach House, 1977), n. pag.

¹²bpNichol, *Journal* (Toronto: Coach House, 1978), p. 69.

¹³Ann Mandel, "Uninventing Structures: Cultural Criticism and the Novels of Robert Kroetsch," *Open Letter*, Third series, No. 8 (1978), 54.

¹⁴"A Conversation with Margaret Laurence," in *Creation*, ed. Robert Kroetsch, James Bacque, and Pierre Gravel (Toronto: new, 1970), p. 53.

[15] Donald Cameron, *Conversations with Canadian Novelists*-Vol. 1 (Toronto: Macmillan, 1973), pp. 91-92.

[16] Cameron, p. 85.

[17] Russell M. Brown, "An Interview with Robert Kroetsch," *University of Windsor Review*, 7 (Spring 1972), 7.

[18] Jay Cantor, *The Space Between: Literature and Politics* (Baltimore: Johns Hopkins Univ. Press, 1981), p. 19.

[19] Wallace Stevens, *The Collected Poems* (New York: Knopf, 1964), p. 355.

[20] Cantor, p. 57.

[21] Jacques Derrida, "Structure, Sign and Play in the Discourse of the Human Sciences," in *The Language of Criticism and the Sciences of Man*, ed. R. Macksey and E. Donato (Baltimore: Johns Hopkins Univ. Press, 1970), p. 256. All further references to this work appear in the text.

[22] Robert Kroetsch, *Gone Indian* (Toronto: new, 1973). All further references to this work (*GI*) appear in the text.

[23] Robert Kroetsch, *The Studhorse Man* (Markham, Ont.: PaperJacks, 1977), p. 133.

[24] Kroetsch, *The Studhorse Man*, p. 39.

[25] Hayden White, "Michel Foucault," in *Structuralism and Since: From Lévi-Strauss to Derrida*, ed. John Sturrock (Oxford: Oxford Univ. Press, 1979).

[26] Robert Kroetsch, *Alibi* (Don Mills, Ont.: Stoddart, 1983), p. 130. All further references to this work appear in the text.

[27] Vonnegut, pp. 22, 24.

CHAPTER FOUR: CANADA: ATWOOD AND DAVIES

[1] Robertson Davies, "The Canada of Myth and Reality," in *Canadian Literature in the 70's*, ed. P. Denham and M. Edwards (Toronto: Holt, Rinehart and Winston, 1980), p. 10. All further references to this work appear in the text.

[2] Graeme Gibson, ed., *Eleven Canadian Novelists* (Toronto: House of Anansi, 1973), p. 8.

[3] Margaret Atwood, *Survival* (Toronto: House of Anansi, 1972), p. 15. All further references to this work appear in the text.

[4] W. H. New, "Modern Fiction," in *Read Canadian*, eds. R. Fulford, D. Godfrey, and A. Rotstein (Toronto: James Lewis & Samuel, 1972), p. 219.

[5] Fulford et al., p. 273.

[6] Quoted in "The Canada of Myth and Reality," p. 14.

[7] Northrop Frye, *The Bush Garden* (Toronto: House of Anansi, 1971), p. vii. All further references to this work appear in the text.

[8] Linda Sadler, "Interview with Margaret Atwood," *The Malahat Review*, No. 41 (Jan. 1977), p. 9.

[9] Joyce Carol Oates, "A Conversation with Margaret Atwood," *Ontario Review*, No. 9 (Fall 1978–Winter 1979), p. 17.

[10] Margaret Atwood, *Life Before Man* (New York: Fawcett Popular Library, 1979), p. 11.

[11] Rosemary Sullivan, "Breaking the Circle," *The Malahat Review*, No. 41, p. 40. All further references to this work appear in the text.

[12] Tom Marshall, "Atwood Under and Above Water," *The Malahat Review*. No. 41, p. 93.

[13] Margaret Atwood, *The Journals of Susanna Moodie* (Toronto: Oxford Univ. Press, 1970), p. 62. All further references to this work (*JSM*) appear in the text.

[14] Marshall, p. 93.

[15] Margaret Atwood, *The Edible Woman* (Toronto: McClelland and Stewart, 1973). All further references to this work (*EW*) appear in the text.

[16] Margaret Atwood, "This Is a Photograph of Me," *The Circle Game* (Toronto: House of Anansi, 1966), p. 11.

[17] Margaret Atwood, *Power Politics* (Toronto: House of Anansi, 1971), p. 37.

[18] Margaret Atwood, *Bodily Harm* (Toronto: McClelland and Stewart, 1981). All further references to this work (*BH*) appear in the text.

[19] Margaret Atwood, "Progressive Insanities of a Pioneer," *The Animals in That Country* (Toronto: Oxford Univ. Press, 1968), p. 39.

[20] Sadler, p. 26.

[21] Margaret Atwood, *Surfacing* (Markham, Ont.: PaperJacks, 1973), p. 7. All further references to this work appear in the text.

[22] Adrienne Rich, "Snapshots of a Daughter-in-Law," in *Adrienne Rich's Poetry* (New York: Norton, 1967), p. 25.

[23] Margaret Atwood, *Lady Oracle* (Toronto: Seal, 1977), p. 25.

[24] Elspeth Buitenhuis, *Robertson Davies* (Toronto: Forum House, 1972), p. 71.

[25] Donald Cameron, ed., *Conversations with Canadian Novelists*, Vol. 1 (Toronto: Macmillan, 1973), p. 33.

[26] Cameron, p. 32.

[27] Robertson Davies, *Fifth Business* (Markham: Penguin, 1977), p. 25. All further references to this work (*FB*) appear in the text.

[28] Robertson Davies, *A Mixture of Frailties* (Toronto: Macmillan, 1958), p. 16.

[29] Davies, *A Mixture of Frailties*, p. 51.

[30] Robertson Davies, *Leaven of Malice* (Toronto: Clarke, Irwin, 1964), p. 172. All further references to this work (*LM*) appear in the text.

[31] Cameron, p. 32.

[32] Robertson Davies, *The Manticore* (Markham: Penguin, 1976), p. 61. All further references to this work (*M*) appear in the text.

[33] Robertson Davies, *World of Wonders* (Markham: Penguin, 1977), p. 287.

[34] Robertson Davies, *The Rebel Angels* (Markham: Penguin, 1982), p. 181.

[35] Davies, *The Rebel Angels*, p. 61.

[36] Davies, *World of Wonders*, p. 225.

[37] Alexander Cockburn, "The Natural Artificer," *The New York Review of Books*, 23 Sept. 1982, p. 22.

CHAPTER FIVE: CONCLUSION

[1] Kathleen Burke, "Review of *Dancing Girls and Other Stories*," *The Review of Contemporary Fiction*, Fall 1983, p. 224.

[2] Edward Said, *The World, the Text and the Critic* (Cambridge, Mass.: Harvard Univ. Press, 1983), p. 30.

[3] Pamela Major-Poetzl, *Foucault's Archaeology of Western Culture: Toward a New Science of History* (Chapel Hill: Univ. of North Carolina Press, 1983), p. 43.

[4] Report of the Commission on the Humanities, *The Humanities in American Life* (Berkeley: Univ. of California Press, 1980), p. 4.

Selected Bibliography

For anyone interested in the comparative study of contemporary fiction in English Canada and the United States, the following items may be of interest. This is not a comprehensive bibliography. It does list the works of the major figures discussed in the preceding pages. More important, it cites writers who and titles which relate to the focus of *A Tale of Two Countries*.

CONTEMPORARY AMERICAN FICTION

Robert Coover's first novel, *The Origin of the Brunists*, won the William Faulkner Award in 1966. His other novels to date are *The Universal Baseball Association, Inc.: J. Henry Waugh, Prop.* and *The Public Burning*; novellas including *Spanking the Maid*, "which he calls a novel," and *Charlie in the House of Rue. Pricksongs and Descants* is a collection of stories, *A Theological Position* a collection of plays. His essay on Samuel Beckett, "The Last Quixote," appears in *New American Review*, No. 11, 1971 (pp. 132–43). Coover contributed a short introduction to the Fiction Collective's *Statements 2*; he has also reviewed two novels of Robert Pinget in *The New York Times Book Review*, 25 Sept. 1983.

William Gass's one novel is *Omensetter's Luck*, his novella, *Willie Master's Lonesome Wife*, his collection of short stories, *In the Heart of the Heart of the Country*. Two collections of essays, *Fiction and the Figures of Life* and *The World within the Word*, contain articles first printed, for the most part, in *The New York Review of Books* to which Gass often used to contribute. Selections from *The Tunnel*, a novel in progress, have appeared in *Fiction* and *Salmagundi. On Being Blue* is a speculative philosophical inquiry on the colour blue.

Other notable writers of experimental fiction, of metafiction, include John Barth, a few of whose novels are *Giles Goat-Boy*, *The Sot-Weed Factor*, *Letters*, and *Sabbatical: A Romance*. A collection of stories is called *Lost in the Funhouse: Fiction for Print, Tape, Live Voice*. Two essays of Barth's on contemporary literature are "The Literature of Exhaustion" (*Atlantic*, Aug. 1967, pp. 29–34) and "The Literature of Replenishment: Postmodernist Fiction" (*Atlantic*, Jan. 1980, pp. 65–71). Donald Barthelme's innumerable short stories are collected in, among others, *Sixty Stories*, *Sadness*, and *City Life*. *Snow White* and *The Dead Father* are novels he has written. *Guilty Pleasures* contains a salmagundi of stories and essays. Thomas Pynchon's three novels to date are *V.*, *The Crying of Lot 49*, and *Gravity's Rainbow*. Among John Hawkes's novels are *The Lime Twig*, *The Blood Oranges*, and *The Passion Artist*.

Other experimental writers who are less well known but whose work is engaging are the following: William Gaddis (*The Recognitions, JR*), Gilbert Sorrentino (*Mulligan Stew, Aberration of Starlight*), Don DeLillo (*End Zone, The Names*), Raymond Federman (*Double or Nothing: A Real Fictitious Discourse, The Two-fold Vibration*), Walter Abish (*Minds Meet, How German Is It: Wie Deutsch Ist Es*), Ronald Sukenick (*98.6, Up*), Max Apple (*The Oranging of America and Other Stories*), Stephen Millhauser (*Edwin Mullhouse: The Life and Death of An American Writer, 1943–1954 by Jeffrey Cartwright*), Alan Friedman (*Hermaphrodeity: The Autobiography of a Poet*).

Interviews with many of the above writers can be found in *The New Fiction: Interviews with Innovative American Writers* by Joe David Bellamy and *Anything Can Happen: Interviews with Contemporary American Novelists* which is edited by T. LeClair and L. McCaffery. The Fiction Collective whose distributor is George Braziller, Inc. publishes a good many experimental works that are thought not to be commercially viable, but are thought to be interesting. *TriQuarterly* has also published many of the above writers in its series called "Ongoing American Fiction."

Critical discussion of contemporary American fiction in books and articles has been voluminous. *Modern Fiction Studies* undertakes periodically to review many of the books on the topic; so too does *Contemporary Literature*. Those works hostile to metafiction are John Gardner's *On Moral Fiction*, Gerald Graff's *Literature Against Itself*, and Mary McCarthy's *Ideas and the Novel*. More laudatory works include Ihab Hassan's "POSTmodernISM: A Paracritical Bibliography," in his *Paracriticisms*, Philip Stevick's *Alternative Pleasures: Post-Realist Fiction and the Tradition*, Raymond Federman's *Surfiction: Fiction Now and Tomorrow*, Tony Tanner's *City of Words*, and Albert J. Guerard's "Notes on the rhetoric of anti-realist fiction" (*TriQuarterly, 30*).

CONTEMPORARY CANADIAN FICTION

Margaret Atwood has published a great deal of fiction and poetry. Her fiction titles include *The Edible Woman*, *Surfacing*, *Lady Oracle*, *Life Before Man*,

Bodily Harm, Dancing Girls and Other Stories, and *Bluebeard's Egg*. *Survival: A Thematic Guide to Canadian Literature* contains her major statement on Canadian literature.

Robertson Davies' novels include the Salterton trilogy (*Tempest-Tost, Leaven of Malice, A Mixture of Frailties*), the Deptford trilogy (*Fifth Business, The Manticore, World of Wonders*), and *The Rebel Angels*. *One Half of Robertson Davies* contains a pot-pourri of essays, including "The Canada of Myth and Reality."

Alice Munro (*Something I've Been Meaning to Tell You... Thirteen Stories*), Margaret Laurence (*A Jest of God, The Fire-Dwellers*), Mordecai Richler (*The Apprenticeship of Duddy Kravitz, Joshua Then and Now*), Hugh Hood (*Black and White Keys*), and Rudy Wiebe (*The Temptations of Big Bear, The Mad Trapper*) are other major Canadian writers who work for the most part in the realistic mode.

Robert Kroetsch has written the following novels: *But We Are Exiles, The Words of My Roaring, Badlands, The Studhorse Man, What the Crow Said, Gone Indian*, and *Alibi*. A number of his essays have been collected in *Robert Kroetsch*, a special number (Fifth Series, Number 4, 1983) of *Open Letter*. *Conversations with Robert Kroetsch* and another series of interviews, *Labyrinths of Voice*, have recently been published.

George Bowering's *Fiction of Contemporary Canada* introduces a number of writers who, he feels, are in one way or another distrustful of realistic fiction. So too do Geoff Hancock's *Illusions 1* and *Illusions 2* (both of which are subtitled "Fables, Fantasies and Metafictions"). Sheila Watson, who wrote *The Double Hook* in 1959 and is regarded by a number of Canadian critics as being in the postmodernist camp, is included. So, too, are David Godfrey whose *The New Ancestors* is regarded similarly, Daphne Marlett (*The Story, She Said*), Audrey Thomas (*Blown Figures*, an unjustifiably ignored novel), Ray Smith (*Cape Breton Is the Thought-Control Centre of Canada*), David Young (*Incognito*), Matt Cohen (*Columbus and the Fat Lady and Other Stories*), and Bowering, himself (*Flycatcher and Other Stories*). Robert Allen's *The Hawryliw Process*, Michael Ondaatje's *The Collected Works of Billy the Kid: Left-Handed Poems*, W.P. Kinsella's *Shoeless Joe Jackson Comes to Iowa*, and Leonard Cohen's *Beautiful Losers* are other experimental novels of note. Quadrant Editions also publishes a good many works by young experimental writers. Two that have recently been published are *The Growing Dawn* by Mark Frutkin and *Backyard Gene Pool* by Ken Decker.

Traditional discussions of Canadian literature in addition to *Survival* include Northrop Frye's *The Bush Garden*, Ronald Sutherland's *Second Image*, D.G. Jones's *Butterfly on Rock: A Study of Themes and Images in*

Canadian Literature. In addition to Robert Kroetsch's incisive essays on the topic, less traditional examinations of Canadian literature and criticism include the following: George Bowering's "Modernism Could Not Last Forever" (*Canadian Fiction Magazine*, No. 32–33 [1979–80]); Frank Davey's "Surviving the Paraphrase" (*Canadian Literature*, No. 70 [1976], pp. 5–13.); Barry Cameron's and Michael Dixon's "Minus Canadian" (*Studies in Canadian Literature*, Summer 1977); John Moss's "Bushed in the Sacred Wood" (*The Human Elements*, Second Series, ed. David Helwig); Louis K. MacKendrick's "Robert Kroetsch and the Modern Canadian Novel of Exhaustion" (*Essays on Canadian Writing*, No. 11 [1978], pp. 10–27). Matt Cohen, whose novels (especially *The Sweet Second Summer of Kitty Malone*) have been called postmodernist, wrote "The Rise and Fall of Serious CanLit: The Golden Years May Be Over" (*Saturday Night*, May 1979, pp. 39–42) in which he assessed the sensibilities of the major novelists in Canada as being Victorian.

Canadian Fiction Magazine publishes interviews with Canadian writers. *Conversations with Canadian Novelists*, vol. 1 and vol. 2, by Donald Cameron, also contain interviews with Canadian authors. In addition to publishing articles on Canadian fiction, *Essays on Canadian Writing* contains lengthy reviews on Canadian fiction and criticism. The more conservative *Canadian Literature* has a similar focus. John Metcalf is an anthologist and short story writer (*Sixteen by Twelve: Short Stories by Canadian Writers*) who has become increasingly insistent recently that Canadian criticism has overstressed its realistic strain.

Little of a comparative nature has been written about Canadian and American Fiction. *Essays on Canadian Writing*, No. 22 (1981), and the aforementioned essays by Robert Kroetsch deal with the topic. So, too, in part does Edgar Z. Friedenberg's *Deference to Authority: The Case of Canada*.